CHUNGKING LISTENING POST

Author in Lanchow talks with a living Buddha (Ch, I Part II)
Tibetan Holy man is from lamasery of Northwest. Religion was discussed...

Chungking Listening Post

BY

MARK TENNIEN

NEW YORK

CREATIVE AGE PRESS, INC.

A Boy, A Camel and China

ONE AFTERNOON IN THE FALL OF 1944, as refugees streamed through the little Chinese town of Tushan near the borders of Indo-China, a boy came along leading a Mongolian camel. Many curious things had been observed in the endless procession of migrants fleeing ahead of the Japanese in South China—but never a camel.

A Maryknoll missioner who stood at the wayside doling out rice, money and words of comfort questioned the boy, who replied, "I am fourteen years old, Shen Fu. The camel and I are alone."

When the lad was seven, his parents had brought him and the camel to Peiping from the steppes of Mongolia. That year, 1937, the Japanese began their invasion of China and the little family fled from Peiping: they went south and the camel went with them. With the Japanese always pressing behind, they plodded on for weeks and months. They reached Hankow on the Yangtze; then they were pushed down to Changsha, to Hengyang, to Kweilin, to Liuchow. . . . The mother collapsed and died on the way; the father was killed in an air raid. The boy and the camel were left, and they were four thousand miles and seven years from home. "And where do you expect to go now?" asked Msgr. John Romaniello.

The boy replied, "I do not know, Shen Fu: only that I am going away from the Japanese and that some day I will return to Mongolia. If the camel and I have to walk all around the waist of the world, we shall return to our home, where the sheep run free in the highlands."

The priest said, "God bless you," and the boy and the camel went slowly down the dust-silenced road out of town, toward the south.

Introductory

WHEN the rough work on this book was done, copies were sent to General Stilwell and General Wedemeyer to ask their comments. They, too, had lived in Chungking during China's eventful and critical days. They lived close to the happenings of the interesting period treated in the book, and I discussed the episodes of *Chungking Listening Post* with them. And so, in place of the usual preface, I give you their comments on the men and the events treated in this book.

Here and there in China I have run across the Maryknoll Boys, and always met a ready welcome. They never asked me if I were Catholic, Protestant or Buddhist, nor did they even hint that I would do well to give some attention to spiritual matters, a point on which I have always been vulnerable. They just tried to make me feel at home. So when one of them puts out a book, I know that it will be written with a kindly outlook in a spirit of tolerance, it will stick to the truth, and it will not pull punches. The Maryknoll Boys live hard and work hard; they preach service, and they practise what they preach. They have been bombed, shelled, hunted, starved, killed—but in the process they have seen a lot of life and they have kept their sense of humor and their grim determination to do their work. If you like people who have courage and live only for unselfish service to others, you will enjoy reading Father Tennien's book.

Joseph W. Stilwell,

General, U. S. Army.

China is in her ninth year of war. Since July 7, 1937, she has resolutely opposed the armed might of Japan. Cut off from the world during much of that time, without modern industry, and with the bulk of her richest territory in enemy hands, she has never faltered.

There will be many stories told in years to come of heroism and privation, faith and despair, suffering and death during those years. Father Tennien records one facet of the scene—that of the missionaries, who, whenever possible, remained at their posts and rendered assistance to the Chinese people in their hour of trouble.

For three of China's most critical war years, 1942-1945, Father Tennien labored tirelessly to facilitate the work of missionaries, cut off from their home countries—many of them behind Japanese lines. His consecrated work required him to travel widely wherever there was hardship or suffering—to the remote province of Sinkiang, to India to arrange for the care of evacuees, to the scenes of floods and locust pests which added to the devastation and famine created by the war.

A keen observer with a retentive memory and sympathetic understanding, Father Tennien has written an absorbing and illuminating saga.

United States Forces in China have been assisted in many ways by missionaries of all faiths and denominations. Sick or wounded men in remote and inaccessible areas have received their unselfish ministrations. The weary, the heartsick and the discouraged have often been comforted by their cheerfulness and their steadfast devotion.

The Armed Forces in their turn have extended assistance to missionaries in many ways, within the desperate limitations of facilities and supplies. Evacuation, travel and medical facilities have been shared whenever possible. Father Tennien gives some interesting sidelights on this friendly cooperation.

A. C. Wedemeyer

Lieutenant General, U. S. Army.

Chungking, China
14 July 1945

Contents

CHUNGKING LISTENING POST

I . . . Outposts of the Cross

1 . . . Wuchow to Chungking

A NARROW, SUN-WASHED LANE served as the street where our Catholic Mission stood in the city of Wuchow, South China. On the morning of December 8, 1941, this lane was enlivened by its conventional cavalcade of peddlers, junkmen, hawkers, children and passers-by. The day was clear and pleasant, stirring everyone with its beckoning energy. Up on the second floor, in my room overlooking the lane, I was working at routine matter piled on my desk. The radio on the window-sill behind me played so gently as to be almost unheard.

On the narrow street itself, Chinese life went on oblivious of the world. A school of raucous youngsters shoaled in and out of the intersecting alley across the way, impelled by some childish game that continually erupted into a clamor of excited activity. Old women, usually content to vegetate on hearthstone or doorstep during the sultry days of summer and autumn, tilted cautiously along the flagstone alley on fragile bound feet. A weathered junkman jogged expertly through the traffic, a treasury of dirty bottles and battered tin cans clinking and rattling in two baskets swinging from a shoulder pole. Somewhere in the neighborhood a bugle was pouring strained notes into the air with less melody than a rain-pipe might give. A barefoot coolie woman, lithe and strong, demanded passage for herself and two water buckets that dripped their contents in a trail of drops behind her.

My reflections on the stream of everyday life below were broken by sudden words from the radio at my elbow: "We interrupt this program for important news flashes. Japanese planes bombed the American fleet in Pearl Harbor." I turned up the volume to hear: "Japanese war planes are strafing American planes on fields near Manila." Then it came even closer to home when the news was flashed: "Japanese fliers just dropped bombs on ships and planes in Hongkong harbor."

As those first bulletins poured over the air, shocking, thrilling and stunning, in turn, I could never have imagined the effect they were to have on my own life—and in a very short time. They were opening up to me a long road that was to leave the junkmen and peddlers of that little alley of Wuchow far behind. My task was to change from a limited one to one that carried with it a solicitude for all of China.

War, as such, was nothing new to those of us who had been living in the Orient. It had been an ugly, unwanted circumstance of life long before the concussion of Pearl Harbor reached us. Since 1938, Japanese bombs had been rocking the vicinity in which I lived. There were hundreds of little bumpy graves on the hillside, for which bombs, shrapnel and gunfire were responsible. Countless refugees were continuously moving up the West River from Canton and ravaged coastal towns. Ragged, hungry and jaundiced soldiers, the backwash of early fighting in Shanghai, Nanking, the Yangtze Valley and the north, were filling the streets of interior China. New and strange dialects could be heard in the market-places as the flux of uprooted humanity receded into the hinterlands. Yet no one made any great complaint. The inconveniences were part of life, part of the price of living; you got used to the cost, and you were willing to pay.

This new venture of Japan's, however, showed a new aspect of danger. We ourselves were involved too sharply and too clearly to shrug it off with any of the complacency that may have already become part of our make-up. Though the war, swirling in and out among us since 1938, had taken its physical toll of missions and personnel, the Japanese had to recognize that we weren't legitimate targets. Our nationality gave us a neutral status in their war with China. Evidently, though, not all of them were aware of this, for many of us spent our time racing along with the Chinese to bomb-shelters. Now Pearl Harbor made us legitimate enemies, and the Japanese zealously began to include us in their operations.

Maryknoll officials in New York went into action as guns roared and flames leaped out of the Pacific. The work of a generation was at stake, and if anything was to be salvaged, there was no time to lose. Things were already happening with dangerous speed. Fourteen young missioners arrived in Hongkong just before the Pan-American clipper ship that brought them became a casualty. Then they, with thirty others, were trapped in the British colony on the South China Sea. In Kongmoon, behind Macao, Missouri-born Bishop Paschang sent as many of his men as he could to safety and new positions. Hongkong, our sole remaining link with the outside world, had fallen, and we in the interior realized that we were cut off.

The outlook for us in the Orient was dismal, when a radiogram reached me from Maryknoll. It stated: PROCEED CHUNGKING IMMEDIATELY. ESTABLISH DISTRIBUTION OFFICE MISSIONS. CLEAR EVERYTHING THRU CHUNGKING. It was the assignment to a complex task, that of connecting America with men and missions ringed in by Japanese and scattered all over China. I packed my bags and set off for a job of dangers, thrills, travail and trouble. With baggage and a motorbike I went to the river and got on a large junk.

Dark came early as the January sun went down on the West River. Little gusts of wet breeze slapped the loose batwing sails of junks along the water front, where sampans were crowded and forests of bamboo poles held torches that flared and winked. In the mat sheds on the wharves, kerosene pressure lamps now added their whistling hiss to the din—the *"shim hoi!*—gangway!" of coolies groaning under their loads and waving split-bamboo torches; the singsong litanies of hawkers and magicians; the hubbub of passengers and their friends bidding them bon voyage; the farewell firecrackers; the sharp liquid cries of boatmen's children; the clamor of pigs and chickens in bamboo crates stacked high on the docks.

I stood on the deck of the river boat to take a farewell look at the city which had been my home since 1928. Departure takes place at the unpredictable time they finish loading the boat, sometime between sunset and dawn. It was shortly after midnight when the wheezing steam launch started to haul us away. Two hundred or more friendly, jovial Chinese crowded the little craft where I was to spend three days and nights on the way to Liuchow. Looking over my baggage marked with the destination in Chinese characters, they remarked, "You go Chungking, so far." Chinese river boats are equipped for leisurely travel. Bunks are fixed on all four sides of the common cabin aft, and people travel reclining. I found my bunk and stretched out with some books I planned to read when people stopped asking me questions.

After three days the boat brought us to Liuchow, the end of waterway traffic. From there on, it was train and truck travel. With rails salvaged ahead of the Japanese advances into North China a new line had been laid from Liuchow more than two hundred miles in the direction of Chungking. After a day on the train I had six days by auto truck through mountainous Kweichow. Twelve other people besides myself, a score of boxes and trunks, and a motorbike bounced up and down. First we were up in the snowy peaks, seven thousand feet high, then down in the green valleys. Gasoline was at a premium, and at the top of each mountain the driver threw the truck into neutral, shut off the gas and let her go.

We came to the crest of the "mountain of seventy-two curves." Seventy-two ribbon curves zig-zagged down the heights, waiting for a painter's canvas, but the view only brought cold sweat to my hands. I crossed myself and put a gigantic task on my guardian angel as I saw several wrecks that had missed the turns. The day before we had had to replace a broken spring, and this left us without a spare. Speeding over the bumps and holes that morning, the front spring went again. After about two hours, the axle broke and the truck nosed into the gravel, while the front wheel ran up the road a quarter of a mile. Another truck was sent to take over the load, and we finally got to Chungking two days late.

Chungking lay across the swift-running Yangtze, which starts in the snows of Tibet. The main city was built on a rock-hill peninsula wedged between the Yangtze and the Chialing rivers. Quarreling coolies swarmed the ferry, racing to take the passengers' baggage. I engaged one to carry baggage and guide me to the T'ien Chu T'ang, Catholic Mission. He gave a side glance at another coolie which seemed to say, "Is this foreign devil in his right mind?"

The coolie turned up T'ien Chu T'ang Kai, Cathedral Street, and I looked for the mission. The coolie suddenly stopped in the middle of the block, in front of a pile of rubble and timbers.

"Here we are," he said, while I stared in amazement at ruins that had once been a cathedral.

"Isn't there another church near here?" I asked.

He shook his head—it might have meant yes or no—and started off with the baggage.

Far in the distance was a high tower with a cross. When we got there I saw that this church was also destroyed by Japanese bombs, and only the tower remained standing. Chinese soldiers were living in the tower, and I asked them where there was another Catholic church.

"Back to the first turn left, then down six blocks, and you'll find Sheng Mo T'ang (St. Mary's Church)," they answered. The coolie was earning money lugging the baggage around, so he kept quiet. When we got to St. Mary's we found only the ruins of a church that had been destroyed once, rebuilt and destroyed again. Living in the ruins of St. Mary's was a watchman. He told us how to get to the Bishop's house, and when I questioned him, assured us that he still had a house.

The Chungking vicariate (or diocese) then comprised some 50,000 faithful served by a score of French missioners and fifty-five Chinese priests. At its head was the extraordinary little man who took me in out of the fog and gave me an unforgettable welcome—the Most Reverend Louis Jantzen. As it turned out, he had been expecting me. He personally answered my knock at his door, which he opened wide in a typical gesture of Latin hospitality. He greeted me with a spate of Gallic rhetoric that immediately put me at ease.

"*Alors, bon jour, bon jour, Père Tennien! Vous êtes arrivé, enfin! Comment ça va?*" You would have thought that we had been friends for years and that I had just come back from a trip.

When he took me to my room—the room which was to serve as my home and headquarters for the next three months —he made voluble apologies. "A thousand pardons," he kept repeating as he showed me where the plaster had been shaken off the walls by bomb concussions and where a hole in the ceiling had been imperfectly patched up. To me, of course, this eight by ten foot cubicle, with a good hard bed and a sturdy ebony chest of drawers, was like a suite at the Ritz.

After I had unpacked and rested briefly, Bishop Jantzen showed me how close his house had come to suffering the same fate as the three churches: one of the walls was propped up on the outside by poles. "If you have to lean against that wall from the inside, *mon père*, lean gently." He smiled. He did not speak much of the horror-filled summers of 1940 and '41, when the Mikado's airmen used Chungking for bombing practice almost at will, but his natural acting ability came into play when he spoke of how the nightmare had been finally brought to an end by *les Américains*—General Chennault's Flying Tigers. "We are enchanted to have another American with us," he said. "Tomorrow you will meet more of them."

In a place like the Chungking of those days you met people quickly, and I soon learned that my host was known and beloved by virtually the entire population, native and foreign. Every evening he received visitors, announced and unannounced, at any time up to nine-thirty. He would rise from his lunch to hear the complaint of the poorest coolie.

In the summer he went out into the field on mission business, and his hardihood is legendary. "He can outwalk the youngest, toughest man in the vicariate," a fellow missioner told me. "Last summer in three months he walked fifteen hundred miles on a confirmation tour, over those jagged ridges that you see in the south and east." On another journey the bishop fell sick with dysentery, and the two young priests at the station insisted that he rest while they found coolies with a sedan chair to carry him. "You will do no such thing," he stormed. "I will be carried when I am dead, not before."

As a matter of fact, he had never wanted to be a bishop at all. Twenty years earlier, when Rome had vested him with the dignity, he wrote a long letter, filled with flourishes and humility, declining the honor. The Supreme Bishop ignored this, however, and urged him to fix a date for his consecration. Again he wrote a respectful letter declining the purple mantle. The Holy Father then sent him a third, terse communication: if he were not consecrated as arranged, Louis Jantzen would be suspended *in sacris*—even the right to say Mass would be taken from him. Thus the humble son of Vosges peasants was literally forced to become a bishop.

2 . . . An Irish Pass

THE TELEGRAPH OFFICE in Chungking was in a modern one-story building of split, woven bamboo cemented over with plaster which was lampblacked against air raids. I flashed news of my arrival to Maryknoll on the Hudson, and as soon as my location was known at home I began receiving frantic messages from relatives and friends seeking to get in touch with other Americans stranded in different parts of China. I determined to answer them as promptly and as fully as possible, and thus my assignment developed new aspects right from the start.

My job was to find ways of getting money, food and medicaments to the hundred and fifty Maryknoll missioners scattered throughout Free China, and so far as possible to assist other missioners also: there were more than fifteen hundred Catholic missioners, seven hundred of them Chinese, in the unoccupied territory. I saw the possibility of forming a network to report the impact of war on the missions and to link stranded Americans with their people at home. Seeking a quick, economical news outlet, I took my problem to Jim Stewart, who broadcasted daily from the war capital's radio station, XGOY. (In addition to his C.B.S. newscast, he was then also filling in for Ted White with *Time* and *Life*.)

I told him I would be forwarding funds to fifteen hundred priests of many nationalities in every part of Free China and that they would be constantly writing me; that I expected to hear from prisoners in internment camps, from men ringed by

Japanese armies, from men hiding in the hills. "I think you've got something there, padre," said Jim. "What you need is a foreign correspondent's card, so you can use the cheap press rate."

That was easy to solve: Maryknoll publishes a monthly magazine, *The Field Afar*. Jim helped me word a radiogram to Bishop Walsh, and twenty-four hours later his reply appointed me correspondent. The Chinese Ministry of Communications granted me a press pass, and I went to work. The priest-correspondent with coat tails flying over the back wheel of his motorbike became a familiar sight in Chungking's steep, muddy streets—especially between the French bishop's house and the radio station.

One day near the press hostel I took a spill that tore my trousers and bruised my leg—just as Harrison Foreman and Pepper Martin came around the corner. They got a big laugh out of seeing me limp into the dispatch room, and one of them declared, "That ain't no motorcycle, it's a murdercycle." The nickname stuck, and thereafter I was often referred to as the padre and his murdercycle. The machine became the object of much envy. Foreman frequently stole a ride on it while I was in the radio station sending a dispatch, and several other correspondents kept after me to sell it at my own price. I had to tell them it was worth more than a Flying Fortress to me, for without it I would never have been able to cover my beat.

But what the newsmen came to envy even more than the bike was my network of contacts in every corner of China. Messengers stole through Japanese lines and arrived with worn bits of rice paper on which notes had been scribbled weeks before—and they related all that they had seen on the road. Missioners escaped from concentration camps and either came to see me or wrote to me. Letters and telegrams from everywhere piled up daily on my desk. Some of the correspondents followed me around like bodyguards, pleading for the exclu-

sive stories which I was dispatching both for the Catholic press
and for syndicated news services throughout America. Once in
a while I was able to give them a break (well after I had filed
my own dispatch, of course).

The Japanese General Staff did not like the sound of my
radio dispatches, which they were intercepting. They wanted
to stop the embarrassing reports—about Japanese soldiers' looting and destroying mission properties—which missioners everywhere were writing to me and I was dispatching to America.
I knew altogether too much.

The invaders put me on the list sent to their spies in China,
offering ten thousand dollars American for my capture. Tai-li,
head of China's secret police, got a copy of the list and showed
it to a friend of mine. It was nice to know I was worth so much
money to somebody, and my life became quite thrilling now
that it was protected by secret police and sought by spies.

Station XGOY allowed each correspondent to send a fifteen-
hundred-word report once a week: it was read at times in a
bombproof studio, located in a cave beneath the city, and
picked up by a California station, where a record of it was
made and airmailed to the writer's news service, paper or
magazine. In this way, during the first few weeks, I was able to
send a number of exclusives on missioners' experiences in
battle-torn Hongkong. Some of the details were smuggled
across the bay and into Free China by Chinese, but the fullest
report came from the Reverend J. Moran, of the Irish Jesuit
Fathers. He was allowed to quit Hongkong because of his neutral nationality.

The scholarly Jesuits—Fathers Cooney, Casey, Kennedy,
Gallagher, Sullivan, Ryan and the rest of them—gave the term
Fighting Irish a new luster during the colony's three-week
siege. They came out of their classrooms rolling up their sleeves
and took up battle posts all over the great mountain that is
Hongkong. Some went up to the Peak, the eyrie of millionaires

which some say commands the most superb view on earth. It was a multiple gun emplacement now, and the priests were bombed out of every chapel they set up, but they stuck it out to the last. Others went to the water front, trying to calm the trapped, fear-crazed crowds. Still others brought the Host right up to the barbed wire alongside the young Canadian defenders, while some wandered about the city, succoring whomever they could.

One day at Des Voeux Road and Peddar Street a priest heard someone call, "Hey, Father!" above the general racket. Pausing, he saw that he was being hailed by a Canadian M. P. who stood directing traffic at the central intersection. Both pedestrian and motor traffic was heavy, in spite of the thick Japanese shell-fire in the Wanchai district a few blocks west. Civilians stepped along as briskly as if they were in New York, and ragamuffin newsboys sprinted in and out of the crowds, hawking their papers with shrill, enthusiastic cries.

The M. P. said, "Father, I would like to go to confession. You see, the last time was . . . in Montreal." The priest smiled. "Right here will do," he said. And the young soldier made his peace on Hongkong's main thoroughfare, at the same time directing traffic and smartly saluting officers as they passed.

This incident was not unusual. Since the beleaguered troops couldn't leave their posts for church, the Jesuits brought the Church to them. On Christmas morning a priest said Mass in the auditing department of the government treasury offices on the fourth floor of the Windsor Hotel; then he went to the roof of the adjoining building and gave Holy Communion to members of an anti-aircraft crew dueling with Japanese dive-bombers. A bomb concussion caused another priest, returning from a similar mission atop the Gloucester Hotel, to lose his grip on a perpendicular fire escape; he seized the ladder again five rungs below and saved himself from a hundred-foot drop.

After the capitulation of Hongkong these valiant men found themselves out of work. Their schoolrooms had been wrecked and their students dispersed. They sent word to their old friends, the Maryknoll Fathers, that they were looking for some occupation—and messages came back from Chungking, Kweilin, Wuchow and Loting, urging them to come quickly. They joined the wave of refugees and trekked wearily over the trails for days or weeks to join the various Maryknoll bishops in Free China. They have been there ever since, carrying on their relief work and church work.

The conquering Japanese lost no time in interning the American missioners at Hongkong, and reports of their valor and sufferings soon began flowing into my Chungking listening post. Some of these stories, particularly the remarkable feats of Father Bernard Francis Meyer, the former Iowa plowboy, have already been related in part.* But the extraordinary adventure of Father Maurice A. Feeney of Albany remains to be told.

Father Maurice Feeney had been caught in Hongkong on the way home for his decennial furlough, and was not rounded up with the other Maryknoll priests because he was temporarily stationed as chaplain at the Maryknoll Sisters' school. He knew that all foreigners were required to procure identity cards, but no one bothered him for the first few days as he went to and fro in the streets. So he reasoned with Celtic logic, "If I apply for a card, I will be interned and become useless. So long as no one notices me I can at least go on with my duties."

A week passed; then two. A month passed. The sentries showed no interest in the quiet, innocent-eyed missioner. Whenever he went across the bay to Hongkong proper or through sectors where guards were numerous, he accompanied one of the Italian fathers from Milan, who flourished his pass

* *Men of Maryknoll*, by James Keller and Meyer Berger. Scribner's, 1944.

as they walked by sentries. The Italian fathers had been interned by the British, but they were set at liberty when the Japanese took Hongkong. Probably the guards thought he was an Italian missioner, or one of the Irish Jesuits still at liberty. This gave the thirty-year-old New Yorker an inspiration: why not apply for a pass allowing him to leave Hongkong for Free China, as some of the neutral Irish missioners had done? He told Bishop Valtorta of Hongkong about his plan.

"You'll never get a pass. It is folly to try," said the Bishop.

But he was not easily discouraged and asked one of the Italian fathers to go with him to the Hongkong branch of the Japanese Foreign Office. The Italian priest carried his identity card in his hand, and they walked past each sentry with a courteous bow and a smile. When they were ushered in to the secretary in charge, they walked up to his desk.

"*Ohaiyo, sinsai*—good morning, sir," Father Feeney said, putting his application for a pass down on the desk. One glance at the nationality—American—and the official shoved it back to him with a look of surprise.

"*Dekillanai*—impossible!" he declared.

"Why"—he pretended to be indignant—"you just gave some Irish missioners passes to leave last week."

"Yes, but you are American. The Irish are neutrals."

"But my parents were born in Ireland. Ask anyone here in Hongkong where he is from: you know that the answer is always the birthplace of his father, grandfather or great-grandfather."

The official was of course aware of this custom. He thought a while.

"Do you mean to say you have walked the streets all these weeks without an identity card and haven't been stopped?"

"Why, yes," the priest answered with a casual air.

"I can't understand how the line of sentries around this place did not arrest you when you entered."

The official was a civilian. The Foreign Office men were frequently at odds with the Army and Navy, and he seemed to be amused at the slip of the military.

"I could write you a pass. The Navy might approve it. I doubt if it would get by the Army, and I'm sure the gendarmes would never give it their stamp," the official said, thinking out loud. He smiled and shook his head, amused at the missioner's good luck, then added, "*Ashida kaiou yoroshi*—come back to-morrow for an answer—if you are still out of jail."

"*Arigado, sinsai*—thank you, sir," said Father Feeney, bowing as he left.

Next morning he came back, but the official told him there was no decision. On the third day he found the pass waiting for him. It read: "Father Feeney, American of Irish extraction."

Astonishingly, after he had the pass, every sentry he met challenged him to produce it!

When the *White Silver Maru*, a coastwise craft about the size and shape of a Hudson River boat, left Hongkong on March 6, Father Feeney was in the first-class saloon, his feet resting comfortably on three suitcases. The ship was bound for Portuguese Macao and French Kwanchowan and his ticket was for the French port, but he intended visiting friends at Macao en route. However, his confidence was to receive a rude jar. The exhilaration of leaving gloomy, imprisoned Hongkong was still warming his heart when a Japanese officer of the ship approached and handed him a blank. "So sorry. Please fill out right away." The blank wanted to know his name, age, occupation and nationality. For the last he simply wrote what was on his pass from Hongkong: "American of Irish extraction."

Father Feeney was growing worried at all this procedure, and he wondered if his pass was really going to get him through.

He was still puzzled by the possible implications of all the questionnaires when the ship reached Macao, which was virtually in Japanese control, though nominally Portuguese. It was an overnight stop, and Father Feeney was picking up his suitcases to go ashore when he heard a voice speaking broken English.

"I thought you were going to Kwanchowan." A polite Japanese officer—polite and very broad-shouldered—addressed him.

"I am."

"Then why get off here?"

"I am going ashore for the night to visit friends. I'll be back tomorrow in time to sail."

"Why take your baggage? There is a baggage room on board."

"I need these suitcases on shore." The priest wanted to be ready for any eventuality, any chance to get into Free China.

But the officer persisted: "Why take all three?"

The man from Albany had an answer for this one, too: "Because I need something out of each one." His round blue eyes were beginning to light up with exasperation, but he held his temper and tacked gracefully. "Here, I'll open them up and you may see for yourself what's in them."

"Never mind," grunted the officer disdainfully, and stalked off.

Father Feeney spent the night with his friends, four Maryknoll priests about whom we shall hear more later, and in the morning he was back aboard the *Maru* as he had promised.

Then, before the ship was ready to sail, he found himself entangled in new troubles, troubles that seemed almost insoluble. A Japanese officer he had not seen before blocked his path on deck and snapped, "What nationality are you?"

For a moment the priest was speechless: were they going to send him back to internment with the rest of the Americans in Hongkong? He looked straight at the officer with his dis-

arming blue eyes and answered as though it meant nothing,
"Irish American."

"Where is your pass?" the startled officer asked, refusing to
believe an American could have obtained a pass to leave
Hongkong.

He handed over his Hongkong card with the notation,
"American of Irish extraction."

The puzzled officer stared at it a while, then started to walk
away, saying, "I must show this to my captain."

But Father Feeney was right with him. "Where are you
going with that? I don't want to lose that pass," he said.

"Oh," said the officer, reflecting. "You come with me. Very
sorry."

In a cabin aft, three or four Japanese officers gave the pass
noncommittal glances. The roundheaded captain seated behind the desk took it, then raised a pair of searching eyes to
the priest and spoke in Japanese. Apparently there was something he wasn't sure of, something that had to be cleared up,
something which shouldn't be dallied with any longer. An
interpreter translated: "Where is your passport?"

This was the narrowest strait Father Feeney had yet en-
countered. On his person he had a passport, a good American
passport. Now all he had to do was pull it out and bring down
on his head a typhoon of samurai wrath. These men, he knew
by their eyes, would accept no excuse, consider no justification.
So he stalled. He said, "That pass I gave you is the only thing
required by the Japanese authorities."

The captain rose on his stumpy legs. "Where is your passport? You must have one."

The priest pointed to the card on the desk: "That's all that's
required. A passport isn't necessary."

But Irish obstinacy didn't impress the officer. His eyes
glittered, and his voice had a flat, deadly finality: "Let's see
your passport."

Father Feeney slowly reached into the inside pocket of his vest and produced the tell-tale document. He saw the incredulous look spring into his inquisitor's eyes. He saw the officer pounce on the thin little book and peruse it page by page. He saw him tremble with anger until beads of sweat stood on his low, leathery forehead.

"American!" the man exploded. Then he launched into a machine-gun clatter of Japanese.

Father Feeney suddenly felt tired. "I do not understand your Japanese," he said, and to the interpreter, "Ask him if he speaks English or Chinese." The officer couldn't and the inquisition went on through the interpreter.

"You are an American," repeated the captain.

"Yes, of Irish descent."

"England, Ireland, Scotland, all one country—enemy!"

"No. Ireland in the south is a free state. Neutral."

"Bah!" Then: "Where are you going?"

"Kwangchowan."

"What are you going to do there?"

"Preach doctrine."

"What is 'preach doctrine'?"

"Teach men to adore the true God and save their souls."

This started the captain off again. Ignoring his interpreter, he raved on in Japanese, his short fingers opening and closing on the passport. Father Feeney interposed, "What are you worrying about? I am a Catholic priest, not a soldier bearing arms. Why are you afraid of me?"

The officer got his breath, considered and asked, "How long are you going to be in Kwangchowan?"

"Three, maybe four months."

The captain weighed this, then abruptly turned away. The interview seemed to be over. After a few moments Father Feeney asked the interpreter what about it. "I don't know," replied that worthy. No one moved. The priest reached over the desk. He picked up his passport, then his pass. He put them in his pocket. No one said anything. He walked out. He went back to his seat in the saloon, and no one came to put him ashore.

Soon the *White Silver Maru* slipped out of Macao and plowed southward in the China Sea. For two days Father Feeney was left to speculate: would they let him off the ship or take him back to Hongkong? Would they allow him to debark, feeling they could seize him any time they wished at the French port, which they controlled as they did Macao?

The *White Silver Maru* dropped anchor in the roadstead of Kwangchowan and the priest watched apprehensively as a French police boat put out from shore, paused at a houseboat to take on two Japanese inspectors, then came alongside and was made fast to the gangplank. The inspectors took all passports, his included, and said, "Very sorry," the owners would get them back by calling at the police station ashore.

But would he be allowed to go ashore? He decided not to ask. Instead, he watched until a French functionary came within earshot and said, "May I go with you in your launch?" The Frenchman shrugged an apology—"No speak English"— and kept going.

The priest bit his tongue. Well, it was now or never. He gathered up his suitcases, walked nonchalantly past the seaman at the gangway and trod gingerly down the ladder to the launch. "Do you speak English?" he asked of an officer, who grinned.

"I try."

"May I go ashore with you?"

"Why not. Hop in, *mon père*. We are leaving."

Father Feeney emitted a gusty sigh. "Thanks," he said. "You speak *good* English."

Ashore, he found Father Lebas at the French mission and told his story. Père Lebas spat out a well-chewed toothpick.

"You wait here," he said and flew out the door. Twenty minutes later he was back with Father Feeney's passport. By noon the man from Albany had crossed into Free China.

Father Feeney had worked without letup or relief for ten years and was due for a rest. Today he is at Maryknoll on the Hudson and his hair is gray. But his round blue Irish eyes still glow with a youthful, disconcerting innocence.

3 . . . I Become a Financial Institution

SPRING REACHED UP the Yangtze Valley. Fingers of warm breeze lifted the fog from the heights above Chungking. In the mudbeds below, rice seedlings pushed up their tiny, serried spears, making emerald mats on the dark brown land. But I had little time for poetic thoughts, for I was deep in intricate bookkeeping. My China-wide network of contacts was taking shape, and I was up early and late arranging for the distribution of mission funds sent from abroad.

The annual subsidies for the sixty-two bishops and sixteen hundred or more Catholic missioners in Free China were sent by the national offices of the Society for the Propagation of the Faith in New York. Bishop Jantzen had been appointed to handle this money, but the work of his diocese was heavy and he asked me to act as his fiscal agent. I was only too glad to do so, for this would mean constant communication with reliable men in every corner of the country, which in turn would insure a steady stream of news into my Chungking listening post.

China's ever-changing economic situation now became a matter of vital interest to me. I had to decide whether the various subsidies should be sent in lump sums or installments, and whether they should sometimes be delayed in hope of a better rate of exchange later on. On such decisions hung material gain or loss for the missions. The business agents (procurators) of all the other religious societies had been trapped in such places as Tientsin, Shanghai and Hongkong. Since Maryknoll had set up anew in Free China, we were asked to handle funds for the American Passionists, Dominicans, Columbans, Vincentians and Divine Word Fathers, and for several European societies.

This put us in the field as a sort of international banking house, for in addition to money from the United States, funds came also from Latin America, Canada, Australia, Great Britain and the Vatican. One of the first things I did in Chungking was to acquire a great stock of leaves for my mission ledger, and in this, for the first few months, working late into the nights, I managed to keep the accounts of my sixty-two "branch banks," the bishops. But I was not a banker, and I soon found out I wasn't even a good bookkeeper.

I was inexpressibly relieved on receiving a note from my young Chinese friend, Joseph Yuen. Back in 1929-30 he had worked for me as language teacher and translator. I had then helped him through the Jesuit Wah Yan College in Hongkong, where he finished top man in his class. He had studied accounting and obtained a good position with the Hongkong Government Treasury. Upon arrival of the Japanese, he had gone into hiding. Now he had smuggled out a message asking if I could employ him once again.

Yes, indeed, I sent word back through the underground. I asked him to come as soon as possible and instructed missions along the way to advance him travel money. And one sunny morning toward the end of May, Joseph Yuen stood grinning at my door. Trained in the intricacies of income tax, he soon had my accounts smoothed out. It was good to see his quick, delicate fingers flying over the beads of the abacus, which in China still takes the place of the adding machine.

As agent for the bishops, I was also thrown into the role of investment banker. Many of them operated in danger zones close to the enemy; they had to be ready to run at a moment's notice, and they didn't relish the prospect of hiking through the mountains with their missions' entire yearly support.

Therefore, they asked me to hold their allotments and send remittances as the need arose. Also, they would be glad if I would place their funds at interest or invest them in any way which would prove advantageous to their missions.

It was a frightening responsibility. All I had to go on was the natural conservatism of a Vermonter raised on a farm, brought up to appreciate and appraise values. One of twelve children, obliged to earn my way through school and college, I learned to make a dollar the hard way and to value it.

With the mission funds of a number of bishops on deposit, when the Chinese currency was weakening and inflationary prices rapidly rising, I had to watch the financial and economic trends very closely. The little mite each of the thousands of missions had to depend on could greatly depreciate in value overnight, or could be suddenly wiped out.

Military reverses or rumors and scares often pushed the Chinese currency down in value and startled people into buying gold metal, goods, American greenbacks or U.S. currency Savings Certificates, and these events and movements had to be watched and weighed.

Weakening currency often compelled us to use up the funds on deposit immediately for current needs and to stop further remittances from abroad for a time; and a great number of other measures had to be taken to meet the changing situation.

Good advice was needed in all these negotiations. One of Bishop Jantzen's parishioners, S. P. Wong, graciously consented to become our financial braintrust. He was generally referred to as the Old Banker. In his late sixties, he had retired for reasons of health after thirty-five years of banking in Chungking, and he knew the secrets of every bank and trading company in the city.

His friends said he was ill because he nearly starved himself to death. This was probably true, for although he was rich enough to build a cluster of skyscrapers, he wouldn't pay a dime for a shoeshine—not that he ever needed one, since he insisted on wearing cloth shoes like a common coolie. Stiff with rheumatism, he would slog through the muddy streets in the rain rather than hire a rickshaw, and he would walk all day from bank to bank without lunch.

During one of his sick spells I prevailed on him to enter a hospital for a few days' treatment. "We will foot the bill," I said. "We've got to make you well quickly. We need your help." The second day in the hospital he asked a nurse what he was costing us daily. At the reply, he jumped out of bed and despite the combined efforts of nurse and doctor, put on his clothes and rushed out to tell me he was quite well. "I will not have such extravagance," he said. For as long as I remained in Chungking he stayed on his feet, suffering physically now and then but always brilliantly alert mentally.

We received further invaluable help and advice from K. K. Kwok, head of the banking department of the Central Bank of All China. I had gone to him with a letter of introduction from his brother, George, manager of the bank in my old post, Wuchow. Such a letter means a great deal in China, and K. K.'s office in the war capital was always open to me. No matter how hard pressed, he found time to discuss problems, to give advice or to grant favors. Twice I overdrew the account in making large remittances to my "branches." On each occasion Mr. Kwok covered us with his personal check, then telephoned to say I could "deposit when it becomes convenient."

In those days the old murdercycle was a friend beyond price, since the need of keeping posted on coming economic events obliged me to dash all over the city interviewing government and financial experts. And the expenditure of gas paid off. In 1943, for instance, we learned months in advance that as of June 1 the government would give 50 per cent more than the regular rate ($18.75 Chinese to $1 U. S.) on funds used for relief, education and mission work. I therefore directed the agencies at home to withhold remittances until advised.

Meanwhile, there was on hand sufficient money to supply the missions' running expenses for many months. This money was in the operating fund created by the subsidies which we were holding and investing at the request of the various bishops. I borrowed from this fund for current needs here or there and credited the respective bishops' account with the same interest as the local banks. When the 50 per cent exchange increase went into effect, the funds waiting abroad were called over and the borrowed money was replaced—with over-all benefit to the missions. This maneuver was repeated in 1944, when we again learned in advance that the government would double its exchange bonus on social and church funds, so that our dollar bought close to forty dollars Chinese.

If there were problems in getting money in from abroad, there were greater problems delivering it from Chungking to the ultimate recipients in the field. Some of these, as I have pointed out, were in danger zones near the fighting; some were in isolated and chaotic regions of Free China; others were in areas surrounded or occupied by the Japanese. To reach these missioners we had to indulge in a game of what we might call pardonable smuggling. Many deeds were done in the dark of the moon; many schemes were devised to outwit the unsuspecting sons of the emperor.

On one occasion we had to get funds to Bishop Connaughton, of the Irish Franciscans, whose territory was half in Free and half in Occupied China. His mission was in a city bristling with the bayonets of Japanese soldiers. These kept the neutral bishop under constant watch and questioning—"for his protection." In a smuggled letter he asked us to get subsidy funds to a Father Mannion, stationed south of the Yellow River in free territory. Father Mannion received the money, and his problem now was to convert it from Chinese currency into Japanese Federal Reserve Bank notes for the Bishop's use. The heavily accoutered Japanese guards on the left bank of the river searched everybody who came across, and anyone found smuggling money was summarily dealt with.

But it takes more than a Japanese sentry to outwit the Irish. Father Mannion went to market and bought a herd of pigs. He also hired some helpers, who drove the swine to the river. Then he hired a trustworthy junk master. The pigs were loaded on the wide-bellied craft and ferried across into enemy territory. The Japanese sentry who watched the unloading had nothing in his manual about searching and questioning pigs. He curtly acknowledged the missioner's bow and smile, and Father Mannion drove the happy, squealing herd into the city. Without difficulty he converted the hogs into Japanese cash, and an hour later Bishop Connaughton had enough money to keep his outposts going for several months. Thus the dollar given by Mrs. Murphy or Mrs. Jones in America went through many changes after crossing the wide Pacific: U. S. currency into Chinese National, Chinese National into pigs, pigs into Japanese currency, and so to the bishop, and from him by barefoot runner into the wild hills of the northern province of Hupeh.

Merchants and trading companies in many parts of the land became our enthusiastic fellow conspirators. When we wanted to get funds to a mission in occupied Shanghai, we dealt through a mercantile house with many widely scattered branches. The house smuggled a letter into Shanghai by courier, directing its Shanghai agent to pay a certain sum of Japanese currency to designated intermediaries, who delivered it to the mission. The courier then returned with the receipt and we handed over the Chinese equivalent to the mercantile house, which welcomed this opportunity of getting capital out of Shanghai.

What I marveled at was the trust that Chinese firms and businessmen placed in me because I represented the Maryknoll Society and—as some of them thought—the whole Catholic Church in America. On my mere written request, they would pay out to some remote corner of China the equivalent of several thousand American dollars. Without their aid I could not have accomplished my task; nor could I have succeeded without the co-operation of courageous and resourceful fellow missioners far out in the field.

Outstanding among these was Msgr. Thomas Megan, of the Divine Word Fathers. A bulgy-muscled, big-boned sort of man, with as much originality as he had energy and daring, he had come to China twenty years before from his native Iowa and until Pearl Harbor had labored in Honan and Shantung provinces, north of the Yellow River. He had seen Japanese columns march into town after town, systematically terrorizing, looting, destroying. He had seen them herd away the women and raze the village, leaving only a charred stain on the flat land. Msgr. Megan was not friendly to the Japanese military. He was an outspoken man who bristled indignantly when they were mentioned.

When the radio in his mission house at Sinhsiang told him America was at war, he hurriedly packed a few bare necessities and made for the hills. Later he learned that he skipped out just one hour ahead of a visit from the Mikado's minions, who smashed into his house with diabolical glee, prepared to pounce on this bold priest who had rubbed them the wrong way so many times. Thwarted, they sacked the mission and posted a price on his head. By this time he was weaving his way over mountain trails. He knew all this country: he could map it with his eyes shut; he knew in which hamlets he would find food and rest, and at what point he would be able to cross the Yellow River at night. Eventually he reached Loyang, on the right bank of the river, in Free China. And from this key city he set about matching wits with the Japanese military in order to aid the less lucky souls in the north.

Eighteen hundred "enemies of the emperor"—Chinese priests, foreign missioners and other foreigners—were interned at Weihsien in Shantung. At Kaifeng in the same province a number of American Sisters were held captive. These and others we were able to assist through the enterprise and resourcefulness of Msgr. Megan.

In the evenings when the stars were up and the moon was down he would slip out of Loyang on a bicycle, a bag of currency strapped over his shoulder. At some near-by deserted spot or lonely hamlet along the bank he would hire a sampan, and the boatman would row across where there were no Japanese sentries. He would pedal his way to the nearest mission, drop the money with a whispered word, and wheel his way back to Loyang before dawn.

He delivered Chinese currency, of course. This was always negotiable in occupied territory if the Japanese did not catch you using it; in this area there were a lot of men who, trading back and forth across the river, were glad to exchange Japanese for Chinese money. Once the funds were across, things went smoothly. Spanish, Irish, Chinese, German and Italian priests saw that the money reached its ultimate destination. Msgr. Megan brought them letters and news from the free world, and on his return his pockets were stuffed with messages of all kinds from the occupied territory.

These messages eventually reached my desk. Those in English, French, German, Italian and Chinese I could manage. But a Polish epistle with consonants piled together like a traffic jam stumped me, and I sent back word asking my correspondent to use French or Latin.

It is impossible to convey the joy that these letters brought me. They told me, sometimes after weeks of anxiety, that the plan had not miscarried; that the runner had got through; that a knot of men in a mountain hideout hundreds of miles away would survive. And this gave me a kind of unholy satisfaction such as I used to feel as a youngster in Vermont, when I crept through marshy willows to a forbidden trout preserve, to hook a string of unwary fat fish; or when I played truant from school and stole off to the pasture to ride the Morgan stallion or get bucked off the backs of unbroken colts.

4 . . . Escape from Lishui

FATHER HARVEY STEELE of Scarboro, Ontario, arrived at Chungking in October, 1942, emaciated and weary after a three-month trek across China from the coast. He told a story of missioners in flight ahead of the Japanese Army, which had been aroused by the Doolittle raid. It is one of the epics of mission history during the war.

The night of April 18, 1942, was dark and drizzly. The Canadian fathers in Lishui, Chekiang, rose from their meal and turned on their radio: through the static from London came word that Tokyo announced enemy planes had bombed Japan. Many cigarettes were burned as the tension grew, and the dial was spun from one broadcast to another. One of the fathers even claimed he could hear airplanes overhead, but the others told him the excitement was getting on his nerves.

They had reason for shock and ragged nerves, for they had lived three years in what was one of the most bombed cities in China. In that time never once had they dared to have Sunday Mass after dawn, when Japanese planes daily swooped like hawks over a brood of chickens. Time and again after the bombing they had walked through rubble and the stark jagged walls that were skeletons of stores and homes. They had pulled out wounded and uncovered dead among ruins for three years.

On this night they talked late, picturing the panic in Tokyo after the first raid. The fathers in Lishui were used to ducking into the air-raid shelters with the uneventful regularity of shaving in the morning, while bombs exploded above them.

31

But not Tokyo. It was the unforgettable first blast for them.

This bombing was the exciting prelude in the lives of Catholic priests and sisters in the missions of Chekiang and Kiangsi that spring. It was to grow into a crescendo of soul-stirring experiences for lay people and missioners alike as the months unfolded. Perhaps enemy bombers would use fields in near-by Chekiang, Tokyo reasoned. So within a short time an irate, desperate Japanese army was on the warpath, looking for landing fields the enemy might use. Within a couple of months that army had turned a good number of the Catholic priests and sisters in Chekiang and Kiangsi provinces out of their missions. Canadian missioners from Scarboro Bluff, Ontario; the Grey Sisters from Pembroke, Ontario; American Vincentian priests in Kiangsi; Columban Fathers in Kiangsi—all these had to dodge the deluge of Japanese armed forces that poured into the two provinces after the bombing of Tokyo.

Priests in these missions south of the long-captured city of Hangchow in northern Chekiang heard from Chinese friends and knew from the intensified aerial bombardments that the zero hour had arrived. The Japanese were coming south along the railroad to Kinwha and then toward Lishui. The priests and sisters made quick plans to evacuate to more southern and mountainous positions. They left Kinwha when the fast, on-rushing Japanese were seventeen miles away. At Lishui, to the south and east of Kinwha, the missioners seemed to have plenty of time.

The Canadian missioners at Lishui sent their baggage, typewriters, and so on to Pihu, twenty miles away, then stayed until the last moment, helping the evacuation. It was a terrifying sight. The great crowd—men carrying heavy basket-loads on their *taming* poles, women with babies strapped to their backs, pappoose fashion—moved along at a slow, steady pace until the air-raid sirens started to scream. Then the great barefoot throng began to run like a frightened herd of sheep;

When Bombers Passed

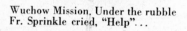

Wuchow Mission, Under the rubble Fr. Sprinkle cried, "Help"...

All that was left of her home...

Ahead: The long road of a refugee.

Author and Chungking cigar speed off to dispatch scoop. Foreman named it a "Murdercycle" . . .

Rice lines start in Shanghai, 1937. American Jesuits were from Calif.

"appy birthday."
ey still wonder
y Fr. Cairns
esn't come back.

ney plodded
ough eight years
war...

her Glass (cap)
wed officials how
boys shoot from
hip...

Lanchow, rendezvous of races. Earringed tribeswoman speaks the old Mongolian tongue.

Smiling tailor from Sinkiang, the province of trouble.

Bespectacled Chinese stone cutter (inset).

Tall hatted Tibetan trader. They fought the Mongols...

Mongolian mother. Her son is a lama at Kumbum lamasery.

Tihwa (Urumchi), Sinkiang capital, city of missioners' torture.

Wheat harvest. High mountains brush the clouds for rain near arid Lanchow...

Buddhist lamasery overlooks village of Northwest.

"Be it ever so humble a yurt is a yurt," say the Sinkiang nomads.

Lanchow to Tihwa 54 cart days. Marco Polo made it...

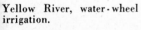

Yellow River, water-wheel irrigation.

Lanchow gateway. Central Asia and trouble straight ahead.

Father Frick, S.V.D. He escaped from cruel imprisonment.

Bishop Buddenbrock, S. V. D., harbored the tortured Fr. Moritz.

Fr. H. Steele, S.F.M., explains to officials. Shrapnel drilled a hole in his hat...

loaded carts and rickshaws overturned; lost children wailed, and old men sank exhausted to the dusty ground.

The Methodist mission, which had the best air-raid shelter in the town, got a bomb plumb center. One hundred and thirty corpses were taken from the ruins. Eventually the city became deserted and silent except for the echo of artillery, now only fifteen miles away.

One evening as the drone of Japanese bombers again grew in the sky, the Chief of Police, himself a parishioner, told the fathers the time had come to get out. The priests notified the sisters, and as soon as the bombers had gone they set out together on the twenty-mile trek to Pihu. All went afoot, including the Mother Superior, who was over sixty. When they arrived, almost blind with weariness, they experienced the first of many disappointments: they would not be able to rest here; the Japanese offensive was greater than anyone had thought, and Pihu was about to be encircled.

At dawn they started out again, leaving their possessions behind. They didn't know where they were bound or how they would get there. There were no coolies to be hired, no rickshaws or sedan chairs for the weary sisters. However, four priests on their way to Lungchuen, eighty miles south, turned up with bicycles and offered their services. Apprehensive yet grateful, the nuns climbed on the basket racks, and the worried priests, now pedaling, now pushing, carried them out of danger.

On the way a violent rainstorm drenched them. One of the priests said later, "We were a sight fit for a comic strip. But what with fighting the slippery mud and thinking of the peril at our heels we didn't laugh. Milton's description of the nun kept running through my mind—'sober, steadfast and de-mure'—hardly appropriate for rain-soaked nuns on bicycles!"

That night they came to a Methodist mission, where the wife of the missionary gave the sisters kimonos to wear while their habits dried out. The following day the bicycling fathers delivered the nuns to the mission at Lungchuen, then returned to Pihu, not yet occupied by the enemy. Here they found among others a priest who seemed too far gone with fever to travel; nevertheless, he was loaded on a bicycle and whisked to safety just ahead of the advancing Japanese.

The refugees were able to rest in Lunchuen a few weeks. Then they were on the move again. And so it went, week after week, down into northern Fukien, then west into Hunan, then south into Kwangsi. Most of the time they went on foot. Sometimes they managed to find bicycles or hitch rides on trucks.

One day one of these trucks was attacked by a bomber, and a sister riding in it clutched a small Chinese child to her breast to protect it as the bombs started falling. The truck turned over, and the sister landed in the mud, still holding the child with her right arm. The child was unscathed, but the nun's arm was broken. A bamboo splint was put on it, and she traveled two days before it could be set.

It was on one of these roads, after leaving Lishui, that Father Steele of Scarboro, Ontario, almost got a piece of his name on his head. The truck in which the young Canadian priest was riding was suddenly attacked one morning by two Japanese planes. The road was flanked on both sides by flooded ricefields. There was no cover. The planes, intent upon destroying the truck, dropped four bombs the first time without touching it or setting it afire. In the meantime, Father Steele had hidden himself under the only cover at hand—the water in the ricefield. There he plopped himself, ten yards from the stalled truck, while the planes came in again for a shot. It was an awkward and dangerous position because, though several inches of water covered his prostrate body, he had to keep his head exposed to get air. Realizing his danger, Father Steele reached under his belly in the inundated mud and pulled out a flat rock a little bigger than his own hand.

Holding it against his ear, he used it to shield his upraised head. It was the luckiest thing he ever did, for the next moment a screaming piece of bomb shrapnel hit it squarely. The middle finger of the hand holding the rock squirted blood into the water. Then the same piece of shrapnel ricocheted, ripping his clerical hat. He now exhibits this hat, saying, "But you see I kept my head."

As all this was happening in Chekiang, the American Vincentians with Bishop Quinn in Kiangsi were watching the situation like worried hawks. But while the Vincentians were looking for developments in the east, something happened that startled them out of their Chinese-made shoes. A new Japanese army from the north and west suddenly rushed down the railway upon them. The bishop, priests, sisters and a group of parishioners escaped to the mountains, where they lived three months until the Japanese army had passed.

The Japanese army that swept in on Bishop Quinn and his personnel from the rear had first gone through the district of Nancheng, where Bishop Cleary and priests of the Columban society were stationed. These men were for the most part of Irish nationality. Father Steele stopped at Nancheng, expecting that the sister's broken arm could be treated there. But in the Nancheng Catholic hospital an American aviator of Doolittle's raiders had not long before been taken in and treated. The Japanese promptly burned the hospital to the ground. The priests and sisters, though neutral nationals, were treated with little respect, for they were foreigners, working to help China, a Japanese officer explained to them.

The Canadian refugees eventually reached the Kwangsi capital, Kweilin, where they were welcomed by Msgr. John Romaniello, a Maryknoller from New Rochelle, N. Y., one of the best-known personalities in the Far Eastern mission field.

Kweilin has often appeared in war communiqués as a key traffic center. But the old walled city, where mandarins once strolled along the river bank under the shade of lacy acacias (the name means Acacia Woods), has known days of much greater importance. Three centuries ago, Kweilin was the provisional capital of China. This was after the conquering Manchus drove the Ming Emperor out of Peking, along with his wife, Helen. Empress Helen had become a convert and was baptized by the Jesuit Fathers, who had been invited by the emperor to teach in Peking. When they had to flee from the Manchus, he took two of the fathers with the court, to Kweilin. In the City of Acacias, nestling under the protection of sheer rocky mountains, the Celestial Emperor built palaces which today stand as tombstones over the grave of three hundred years of history. Here, eventually, the Ming dynasty fell. And here the Empress Helen had set up a fine mission for the Jesuit Fathers, before the Manchu Army conquered the Mings and took Helen back to Peking as a hostage. Mission endeavor in Kweilin ended with the Mings. One missioner left for Rome, and the other was probably killed by the Manchus.

5 . . . Linus Wong the Irrepressible

FATHER JAMES F. SMITH was tired of bowing to Japanese soldiers in Macao, and during his six months' internment as guest of the emperor, he was quietly planning an escape. The Japanese Army had taken Kongmoon, South China, in 1939, but the American priests there went on with their mission tasks and in addition dispensed rice and wheat daily to the thousands of starving refugees. Then Pearl Harbor ended their freedom, and Bishop Paschang and the other three were marched off to the near-by city of Macao. This left only the daring, resourceful young priest, Father Linus Wong, with a cathedral, a seminary and the countryside of Christians to care for as best he could under the heel of Japanese occupation. Father Smith and Father William North, interned in Macao, finally got Chinese boatmen to smuggle them out to Free China. The priests were hidden deep in the hold of a Chinese junk among the freight. They sailed out of the harbor, and at an arranged point on the coast of Free China a sampan took them off. Guerrillas then brought them to the interior, where Father Smith wired that he was free. Work at the Chungking post was increasing, and I asked Father Smith to come direct to Chungking to assist me. He brought with him the story of Father Wong and his daring encounters with the enemy.

Linus Wong, whom I had known in Wuchow, was a go-getter of the Horatio Alger variety. His fellow students of the Kongmoon Junior Seminary had been quiet and subdued, but he was restless, a live-wire, a born organizer. The pranks of his student days which brought the frown of authority upon him and made his stay at the seminary so tenuous were innocent enough. But they were out of place within such walls; moreover, they had a way of turning out wrong either for himself or for others.

There was the case of the chickens. He had figured it out on paper that if each boy raised a hen or two, the student body could help support the school in no time—and pocket enough cash on the side to buy hair oil for all. A few shrewd deals in the village and, presto, the seminary garden was an unsightly mess of upturned cases, each harboring one or more hopeful hens. The rector and faculty looked kindly enough on this project until there was an outbreak of an epidemic of lice, fights and greasy long hair. Lice were natural companions for the chickens and quite in place in a henhouse, but when they began to invade the classrooms and dormitories it was thought the matter had gone far enough. The fights might have been overlooked as an innocent misunderstanding—eggs are after all very fragile things and have been known to vanish into air, and chicks have been known to stray into someone else's coop —but the hair oil was the limit. When the seminary began to smell like an unaired barbershop, the stiff broom of authority swept out hens, roosts, hair oil bottles—and very nearly Businessman Wong.

Then there was an experiment in dog raising, followed by one in tree planting. Neither panned out, and each time Linus almost washed out. Finally came the unhappy affair of the bicycles. During a summer vacation, with time heavy on his hands, Linus became aware of the quick growth of transportation in Kwangtung province and decided to have a share of it. He borrowed some cash, bought a collection of broken-down bikes, patched them up, and, using a couple of town loafers as front men, opened a bicycle-renting business in Kongmoon.

Things went along fine during the summer, when he could

be on the spot and watch his partners. But after school re-opened, the inevitable took place: the straw men flourished, while his dividends dwindled. A few heated arguments over the school fence about profit and loss brought the venture to the attention of the authorities, and this time it seemed certain that Linus would be expelled. But Father Paulhus, though necessarily severe, was particularly gifted with insight. He saw in this Chinese Peck's Bad Boy the makings of a fine man, perhaps even a fine priest, and once more he let him stay. The grateful Linus presented the seminary with his complete stock of broken-down bikes and bent his head in humility and study.

The shock of financial loss, and the self-control of which he found himself capable, kept Linus out of mischief in his final year, and he was graduated to the major seminary in near-by Hongkong. Here he distinguished himself for his application and developed a flair for Chinese composition that got his by-line into the local Catholic press. After completing his seven-year course he became the third native priest in the Kong-moon vicariate, which was staffed by Maryknoll Fathers.

His ordination was held under unorthodox conditions. By this time the Japanese had occupied the Canton delta region, but although they made life complicated for civilians—priests, nuns and Chinese Christians included—they did not stop the ordination ceremony. The cathedral was packed with people who came to see a native son raised to the dignity of the priest-hood, and everything was going along smoothly, when the squat silhouettes of Japanese soldiers appeared in the main portal. This was a signal for the hasty departure of all the women and some of the men. Fortunately the pagan intruders were sober—they had come out of mere curiosity—and even though no one felt entirely at ease, the ceremony proceeded to its inspiring completion.

Father Wong was made an assistant in the cathedral parish.

Because he was connected with Americans, he was inevitably beset by molestation and danger, yet he never lost his cheerfulness and soon became indispensable to Bishop Adolph Paschang. In spite of the fact that America was not yet at war with Japan, American priests couldn't walk a quarter of a mile from the mission without being turned back by a sentry. The Chinese could go about freely, at least in theory. In actual practice every encounter with a sentry was humiliating, often worse. Besides making the usual profound bow and being searched for weapons—and for cash—there was frequently a face-slapping by these soldiers, who were described in Tokyo's tireless propaganda as "your real friends, come to liberate you from foreign slavery." This treatment naturally rankled with all Chinese forced by circumstances to remain in occupied territory and especially with Father Wong, who was never the meek type.

His inventive mind soon hit on a scheme for avoiding these tokens of friendship. He adopted a semi-military dress, appropriated a bicycle (a luxury ordinarily enjoyed only by the Japanese and their satellites) and went forth, head high, neither bowing nor scraping. His bluff worked. To the Japanese sentries, anyone so brazen as to ignore them—the incarnate representatives of the divine emperor—appeared to be a puppet of the first rank. His precious and honorable person must be held in almost sacrosanct regard. As for the puppet troops, they were utterly confused; but putting their money on the winning horse, as usual, they saluted as he sailed by their posts.

In this way Father Wong performed countless services for the mission and took countless chances, often against his superior's advice. To him, each new day was an adventure; his eyes sparkled with the pleasant prospect of putting something over on the slower-witted soldiery. He became a figure in Kongmoon and a golden-haired boy to the money changers, who were always on the lookout for foreign checks. He cashed many of these every week, and his passage down Money-Changer Lane was a triumphant march between shops bidding against each other for his trade. This sort of thing amused him very much, and he used to re-enact some of the more humorous scenes on his return to the mission. At a time when the soldiers were taking every ten-cent piece from the coolies, he rode boldly by with thousands stuffed in his pockets. The fathers used to sigh with relief when he returned for supper. It meant their youngest and best loved was in for the night—he had come safely through one more day.

The worst scare he gave his friends was during the cholera epidemic. The Japanese ordered the mission to stop giving out rice, fearing that the two or three thousand needy who filed in and out of the mission compound daily would spread the disease further. This was right in a way, but then, if the rice dole ceased, those who didn't starve to death would all the more easily fall prey to the epidemic. So Bishop Paschang ignored the command. The Japanese then ordered puppet troops to break up the long rice lines, but this didn't work either—the puppets had no heart for such a job. The third move in this ticklish game of wooden mentality versus charity and nerve was a Japanese warning that the foreigners would be shot if the distribution of food went on. This also the bishop ignored, whereupon the soldiers started beating up the unfortunates en route to the mission. But for once they were up against something stronger than their New Order—a philosophy which said, "It is better to be killed than to starve to death."

Thus the people won the decision, but they almost lost the stake, for the mission's supply of rice ran out. Thousands of bags of American Red Cross wheat and rice were in Canton godowns, ready for consignment to the mission. But getting a permit to bring anything into the mission was out of the question, and once more the incomparable Wong came to the rescue. He simply went into Kongmoon City, hired some

trucks, filled them with rice and brought them into the compound. As usual, he did not bother asking for a pass—merely
waved a blank paper when he went by the sentries.

It was then that Father Wong had another attack of business fever. He figured that by setting up a lot of people in
small shops he would be able to relieve the pressure on the rice
line. He gave away his salary for a year in advance, and
Kongmoon began to blossom with little stands selling cookies,
peanuts and cigarettes. The idea may have been sound enough,
but cash customers were few, and the proprietors were unable
to resist their own wares, being as hungry as anybody else.
Result, no change in the rice line and no change in Father
Wong's pocket. Experiences of this sort cast him into spells
of gloom, but these were often dissipated when the other
fathers asked him to join them in a game of hearts. He had
been taught this innocent pastime early in his career, and he
glowed with fiendish glee whenever he was able to force one of
his former teachers to take the Queen of Spades.

Such games came to an end when America entered the war.
Bishop Paschang, Father Paulhus, several other priests and the
Maryknoll sisters were interned in neighboring Macao. And
here is where Linus Wong really showed his mettle. He could
easily have said, "There is nothing more I can do here, I may
as well go to Free China, where I will be needed." Instead, he
stuck to his post. The mission was taken over: Japanese soldiers
lived in the house, and their horses were stabled in the church.
But there remained the problem of disbanding the schools
where Father Wong had helped teach doctrine and of getting
the boys and girls safely back to their homes in various parts
of Kwantung. The Japanese soldiers were in an ugly frame of
mind, and for the first time in his life Father Wong ate humble
pie to secure passes for the children going to Free China. Then
he personally conducted them to safety in small groups, which
meant weeks of travel.

But he did not stop there. Adult Christians remained in the Kongmoon parish, and he returned to minister to these. In the difficult year that followed, the business rash broke out again, this time for keeps, since mission funds from America had been cut off for the time. He had to find a way to live. A rabbit-raising venture which had been in the back of his mind since boyhood now became a profitable reality. At last he was a business success!

Later, funds from Chungking were available for him. How to get them through the triple threat of bandits, puppets and Japanese soldiers with long memories was a problem that Linus Wong solved in his own inimitable way. Once a month he managed to make his way to a town in Free China where the funds awaited him. Converting the money into small gold nuggets was for a man of his stamp relatively simple. While border sentries were gibing at him and stripping him of the few dollars he had left for them in his pockets, his mouth was full of gold nuggets. Afterward, asked what he would have done if told to open his mouth, he said, "I'd have swallowed them and hoped for the best."

Eventually, as we shall relate, Bishop Paschang escaped from internment. He decided Father Linus Wong had done all that one priest could be asked to do, and more; he took him from his rabbits and his friends and assigned him to a post in Free China. But although he was quartered in relatively safe territory, Father Wong did not lead a safe life. He persisted in running the blockade into Kongmoon, always with some new scheme to aid his brethren in captivity.

6 . . . A Priest among Bandits

WHEN A TELEGRAM TOLD US in Chungking that Japanese army and puppet troops had attacked Chekkai on a foraging raid, none of us worried. We knew Father Donat Chatigny could hide out in some bandit lair where he had been called in the past to cure the sick. A week later we learned he was back at his ransacked mission, with nothing but good to say about the friends who had harbored him in the hills, and nothing bad to say about the enemy who had despoiled his mission. Like St. Francis, who befriended a wolf, Father Donat found some good in everybody.

Father Donat Chatigny was a smallish, bald man, just turning forty, so gentle of mien that one of his flock once said, "He is just like St. Joseph." But though soft of speech, this priest had iron in his courage. And he needed it, for he carried on his labor of mercy right under the guns of the enemy. He was one of those missioners who worked in the front line, in perpetual danger of surprise and capture.

The China Sea runs in and out of a jagged coast line for about two hundred miles between the Canton Delta and French Kwanchowan. That is the seafront of the Maryknoll mission precariously facing enemy-held islands just off the coast. From time to time the Japanese poured a blast of shells into these towns and landed on foraging raids.

Perhaps the most dangerous and nerve-wracking place in that mission field was the peninsula of Chekkai, which stuck out like a finger to taunt the ships that sailed menacingly up and down the coast. This hot assignment needed a man with a clear mind, a cool head and a brave heart. His bishop found these qualities and many more in Father Chatigny, an imperturbable little gentleman who comes from the gentle folk of Acadia and speaks in soft words like "the murmuring pines and the hemlocks."

I first came to know Father Donat during his arts course. The students noted his seraphic smile, soft voice and rapture at prayer, and laughingly called him "Curé of Ars," after the famous St. Jean Vianney. The faculty found that, though his head was in the stars, his feet were on the ground, and he established himself as a leader in studies or in labor tasks assigned. He himself was never ruffled and he never ruffled another by a sharp word.

Chekkai is a mountainous little country where the people speak the Hakka dialect, a language that is strange to the neighboring districts. These Chinese hillbillies are for the most part hard-working farmers and fishermen, but guns hang on the wall of almost every home, and these rough gun-toters have feuds that would startle the Tennessee mountaineers out of their homemade boots.

Catholicism in Chekkai is generations old. The Christians there are not hallelujah-shoutin' revivalists but firm believers, though rough and tough like the mountains and people around them. Once converted, they have little time for those who do not see the light. They are not exactly spiritual snobs, but rather inclined to the attitude of "let the devil keep his own." When the priest went around to help sick pagans, his Catholics sometimes told him he would do better to keep his pills and energies for the faithful of the fold. The little pastor was an enigma to the unlettered working folk of Chekkai. Religion for them was something very necessary to save their own souls, and that was about all. Their religion was tied to the earth, not hitched to a cloud, and it puzzled them to see the good padre helping the Catholic, the pagan, the rich or the poor, the official or the bandit.

For almost a decade the pint-sized missioner with the disarming look about him tramped the bandit-infested mountain paths as if strolling in fields of lilies. He went unmolested, for the bandits respected the man who had love for all and malice toward no one.

On his trips through the country, Father Chatigny carries his Mass kit and a medicine kit, for he is a great healer of bodies as well as souls. His remedies range from old-fashioned ones, dating back to Evangeline's grandmother, to the latest sulfa drugs. He crosses the hills, winds his way through the rice paddies and wades the streams to visit his scattered flock in the distant villages. When others of us fume and sweat in the season of prickly heat, he always seems cool and unbothered and walks along briskly, as if born to the tropics rather than to the snows of Quebec.

Just before the war I made a pilgrimage trip across the water with him to Sancian Island, where St. Francis Xavier died in 1552. When a stiff wind filled the sail, the boatmen swore at having too much wind while they reefed the sails and swung the rudder. Then when the wind died and the boatmen whistled to call up a breeze, between breaths they cursed the devils that had stopped the wind. I myself was worried as the boat tipped and leaped in the high wind and galloping waves, and was impatient with the calm an hour later, which left us in the middle of nowhere. But Father Chatigny took it all with the composure of the rocky coast of his parish.

During the calm they gave us a meal of rice and fish on the boat. Grace before meals is for many of us a perfunctory thing, with a wave of the hand for the sign of the cross. But before this frugal meal Father Chatigny's sign of the cross was a solemn rite, his grace a devotional ceremony such as might precede a Christmas dinner.

But not always is he mild, if always meek. In a sermon at one of his mountain mission stations he was scourging his people, for he heard they had been aiding bandits in a recent raid. The people were squirming and worried and kept staring with horror toward one of the low windows. He looked that way and saw framed in the window the faces of four of the bandits themselves. But while they leaned on their rifles, the fearless priest told his people that banditry was wrong, bad and unjust, and that they should have nothing to do with the bandits. Even bandits admire courage and respect a just man, so there was no shooting.

Tramping through the mountains, Father Chatigny digs up strange flowers and plants and orchids. For besides his orphanage and his dispensary at the home mission, he has a third love—his garden. When he goes to visit a fellow missioner he brings seeds and slips of flowering shrubs and plants. The Flame of the Forest which overspreads his church or the pink bougainvillea which climbs the tower has offspring in all the near-by missions.

Father Chatigny's letters best show the man. A great part of a letter of his often sounds like St. Francis of Sales or the author of the Imitation of Christ; another part will be practical and pedestrian. People turn up at neighboring missions with letters from Father Donat which end like this: "This boy's father is a bandit; keep him away from home, give him a job and work him hard. I am sure he'll turn out all right." Or, "This man is very poor, I can't cure his sickness. Have the doctor do his best and please feed him up." Or again, "This woman was thrown out of her village; ask the sisters to put her to work in your orphanage so we can rehabilitate the poor woman."

Famines, feuds, bombs, shells and invasions fail to excite

the imperturbable little priest. Reassuring words roll out of
him in the tensest situations. One day he was visiting Father
Sweeney's leper colony in the neighboring county of Toishan.
He went to the church in the afternoon to hear confessions.
The Japanese across the river started to shell the place. Two
shells exploded in front of the church. Father Donat slowly
folded his stole and came out of the confessional and calmed
the frightened people milling around the church. With the
other priests he directed the lepers to the sacristy and back
door. Then he helped carry the cripples up an embankment,
across a road and down into a gully. In a few moments a shell
landed smack on the road, and another in the gully. The priest
gave general absolution to prepare the people for death. They
then expected Father Donat to pronounce some elevating and
spiritual thoughts on eternity. But idealists are, after all, the
most practical men, and he calmly sat down, saying, "We are
all ready now, and there is no use worrying; if it gets you, it
gets you."

Through nearly seven years of war Father Chatigny lived
there alone, the only foreigner in the country that looks out
on islands held by the Japanese. He saw their warships come
close and shell, and his bag was always packed for the time
when the enemy threatened to land again. Later he saw the
big bombers with the star and bar—the American emblem—
patrolling the sea off shore. He also saw two Japanese ships
floundering after hits by American bombs. Twenty of the Japanese in a lifeboat were picked up by a big fishing junk and
brought to a coastal village of his fishing folk, where they were
turned over to the local soldiers.

His has been a lonely, wearisome labor during these trying
years. But now he has Father Hoh, a Chinese priest, to assist
him. Father Hoh was completing his studies in Hongkong
when the Japanese attacked the city. He lived through the

siege and later walked nearly two hundred miles into Free China to be ordained by Bishop Paschang.

From Father Donat he will learn about the feuds in the hills, the squabbles of his weather-browned fishermen, the gambling of his varicose-veined, stout-legged coolies, the fights of the gossipy old women and of the incorrigible bandits living in the hills. But he will hear Father Donat conclude, "Oh, but there is so much good in all of them."

Now, with an assistant, Father Chatigny may have more time to holiday in the leper colony or to visit neighboring priests with his basket of flower seeds, shrubbery slips and fruits. They will still smile at his foibles and tease him a little, but he will always be sunshine, for he has found the bright road through this world of war and tragedy, where most of mankind seems to have lost its sanity. He is as refreshing as the dew, for though he walks the earth with us, he walks the high road—so high that his world is carpeted with clouds.

7 . . . A Mystery of the China Sea

ONE OF THE JAPANESE-HELD ISLANDS on which Father Chatigny could look from the tip of Chekkai was Sancian, the desolate, mountainous dot of land where, four centuries ago, Francis Xavier, roving liegeman of the Cross, died lonely and fever-racked. For years this island had been the parish of Father Robert Cairns, whose abduction and subsequent disappearance a few days after Pearl Harbor remain to his fellow missioners the most poignant mystery of the war. All the time I was in Chungking, cryptic reports came trickling in piecemeal, like bits of wreckage and gear floating in from the sea—each message more disheartening than the last. Father Joseph Lavin wrote that after a year of investigation and searching, the priests of the district decided Father Cairns was dead, and they offered Masses for his soul.

Father Cairns was taken off his island mission of Sancian on December 16, 1941, in a Japanese motorboat. His house servant heard the Japanese officer tell the priest that he was to be taken to Kwonghoi, a city eighteen miles away on the mainland. There he was to be turned over to the Japanese gendarmerie as an enemy national. Kwonghoi people say that neither the boat nor Father Cairns arrived. People along the shore found a hat washed in from the sea—it belonged to Father Cairns. The Toishan Magistrate carried out an investigation for the priests of the district. He found that one of the puppet soldiers with the Japanese had later deserted his masters. This soldier confessed that he had helped to do away with Father Cairns on the boat; he said that the priest's body had been cast overboard.

For six months the Swiss consul in Canton pressed the Japanese consul for news of Father Cairns. The Nipponese finally answered that Father Cairns was "interned on Canton Island off the coast." But maps do not show this place, nor can we find out where Canton Island lies. Many confreres wrote to say they were sure the priest was dead. But while we wait for the postwar smoke and clouds to clear and give us the truth, let me tell the story behind these telegraphic messages and letters reaching Chungking.

I had my first view of "Bobby" or "Sandy," as he is called by his intimates, when I first arrived in China, back in 1928. We were at table when a quick-moving Scotch priest rushed in to join us. He threw his sun helmet at the rack, wiped the perspiration from his face and gave us a beaming smile. I knew then I was going to like Bobby.

We had both studied at the same college in his home town of Worcester, Mass., so he came to my room to talk. In the early years of the century the boy Robert Cairns was running a laundry business in Worcester. With a horse and wagon he dashed about the city, earning enough, dollar by dollar, to go to college. After college he went on to study for the priesthood.

One of my last visits with Father Cairns took place late one night in Hongkong, the summer before the war.

A door swung back, letting a flood of brilliant light into the hallway. Father Sandy Cairns stepped out into the corridor. He quietly shut the door behind him, swamping the hallway with darkness again. The unheeled bedroom slippers he wore slid noiselessly along the tiled floor leading to the porch. It was almost midnight, and there was no noise except the restless rhythmic beat of the sea rolling in on the beach below. A few miles away the beacon that marked Hongkong's harbor entrance glowed alternately bright and dim like a wearied torch in some phantom land. Stanley Peninsula, the fortress outpost of an empire, which was, ironically, to become an internment camp for the British, loomed up in the still night like a predatory animal awaiting its prey. My attention switched to Father Cairns, then almost within reach of me.

In the shadow of the porch I gave Father Cairns a mild start when I said, "What are you doing up so late?"

It was only for a second. Then he fell upon me with eagerness. "Come on up to my room," he urged. "I've got a job for you."

Sandy was famed for his enterprise, a quality that kept him as busy as a contractor on a skyscraper job. For him it was recreation to be busy about many things, and in his opinion midnight was as good a time as any for starting a project.

In his room there was a litter of papers, clippings from newspapers from Los Angeles to Boston. They were write-ups on Catholic missions, Francis Xavier, South China and Sancian Island. Many of them Father Cairns had written himself and sent back to American editors and newspaper friends for publication. On his desk was a seven-column, four-page newspaper that gave me the clue to the bustle and energy of Sandy's midnight job. The name *Sancian Times* caught my eye.

"Is this your paper?" I asked in surprise.

"That's the *Sancian Times*," he replied, with the beaming air of a proprietor. "The next edition is spread all about here. You can help me get it together."

Father Cairns was living up to his reputation as an entrepreneur. While the rest of the house slept, he was wide awake and absorbed in the task of beating his own deadline. He was playing editor, reporter, business manager and publisher all at the same time. I paused to wonder at the energy that propelled him, and then I pitched in to help.

Father Cairns' first affection was for that little dot of an island named Sancian, and you'd have to know him to appreciate it. You'd have to know how he went through Holy Cross College in Worcester and St. Mary's in Baltimore, and then to Maryknoll in New York, before coming to China. You'd have to see him on Sancian's crags, high up where a shrine marks the spot on which Xavier died, when storms and squalls are washing in from the Pacific.

The man was proud of Sancian and wanted with all his heart to make it a place of which his church and China would be proud. His enthusiasm sprang out of the strong conviction motivating his life as a missioner of the same God that was Xavier's.

These qualities made him a real companion to his people. He looked upon life as a rich adventure, rich because it was real. It had to do with his Sancian Islanders, and everything he did was aimed merrily at God. Even that night, working on the paper, this spirit marked him. It animated him as he moved about in shabby black trousers, white collarless shirt and dragging bedroom slippers—an outfit that gave a Bohemian touch to his vigor. His white hair, cut pompadour fashion, stood up alertly, and his clear eyes twinkled behind silver-rimmed glasses. Finally, giving me a jubilant clap on the back, he announced, "There you are; the next edition of the *Sancian Times* ready for the printers!"

The next time I saw Father Cairns, he was in Canton. After the Japanese had taken the city, he had come up from Sancian to help the Red Cross people, who were doing famine and relief work in the bedraggled city among the dislocated poor classes. This was before Pearl Harbor, while Americans in Occupied China still enjoyed a dubious status as third nationals.

Although the Japanese had conquered the place, Father Cairns was king in Canton. He made the Red Cross work click. The handling of the all-important rice was his responsibility, and he assumed it easily. Much of his time was spent on the

water fronts, supervising its loading or unloading. The grain
had a readier value than gold, yet Father Sandy arranged
safe delivery to the people for whom it was intended. He was
stevedore, coolie boss, cajoler, diplomat, helmsman and buffer.
Even the Japanese, at least the broader-minded ones, bowed
to his genius for getting things done. The poor coolie's guar-
antee of life in those days in Canton had its symbol in the
short, stumpy figure of Father Cairns. The congee kitchens
were supported and supplied by his untiring devotion to the
poor people he served.

As time went on, Canton slowly and surely became uncomfortable for those whose nationality marked them as not seeing
eye to eye politically with the Nipponese. It was the fog coming in from the ocean of the future, a future that would bring
global war. Many Chinese, feeling this clamminess, surrepti-
tiously left for the interior, trekking westward in long lines to
China's new ramparts. Many of these people carried thought-
ful letters of introduction from Father Cairns to help them
secure work. Even the foreign youngsters in Shameen, to
whom Sandy had been confidant, teacher and pastor, left for
places that many had never seen, waving gay little good-bys.

As he watched the transformation of Canton, as farewells
became more and more frequent, Father Cairns knew his work
there was finished. He felt that the relief work, though it must
still be done, needed his assistance no longer. He went back
to his heart's parish, Sancian.

The island lies in the road that Japanese battlewagons used
to reach points of conquest in the Eastern Pacific and South
China Sea. Trade winds blowing from the northwest gave the
eastern side of the island a rough, rolling surf. A small range
of mountains slopes down to a little bay on the western side,
where the Catholic Mission is, and a sandy, even beach
smooths out the rollers coming in. The beach ends abruptly at

a rocky, bluff-like promontory upon which stands the shrine of Francis Xavier.

The archipelago of which Sancian is the port has a reputation built out of time and legend. Pirating in the adjacent waters has always been a recognized profession. Over the years that Father Cairns and his predecessors lived on the island, the sporadic crackling of sea robbers' rifles was frequently heard. The outlaws, men who took pride in their primitive code, were trustworthy in the sense that their rules insured a left-handed chivalry to victims and a pledge against unwarranted violence. When the so-called "incident" hit South China it started a wave of crime by a new "non-union" crowd of bandits who took their cue from the Japanese desire to create confusion and discontent with the reigning order.

In the days after his arrival from Canton, Father Cairns kept himself busy, not with premonitions of coming trouble, but with plans for a Christmas festival which would bring his fishing flock in from the seas for Mass and Adoration. His capable assistant, Father John Joyce of Forest Hills, Long Island, was on the mainland and planned to spend the feast in a mission over there. So it was up to Father Cairns to prepare everything himself.

On December 8 he was telling the sisters to have the youngsters in shape for choir duty at Christmas Midnight Mass. . . . Hongkong, the Philippines, Singapore, the East Indies, and Burma were under attack. Pearl Harbor, far beyond Sancian's eastern horizon, was even then belching hot smoke. Without radio or any other contact with the world beyond his island, Father Cairns went happily on with his Christmas plans.

On December 9, puppet soldiers landed on the beach near the mission. Bustling and angry, Father Cairns held the looters at bay. Over at the convent the sisters got the signal and ran to the hills. The looters went to the boat and brought back guns. It took several to keep the fighting Scottish priest covered. The others looted his property and loaded it on their boat, to the bewilderment of Father Cairns, who knew nothing of the Japanese-American war.

On December 13, while the morning mist was still on the sea, another boat, armed for action, made a surprise landing. This time the occupants were Japanese. Most of them disappeared over the hill behind the mission, heading in the direction of the villages along the east shore. One lone officer made his way up to the mission to greet the priest austerely, though not without courtesy. It was evident he had something to say, something forthright and weighty.

"You will have to leave this island," he informed Father Cairns. "Japan and America are at war."

Perhaps the officer was a Catholic and wanted to help Father Sandy. At least he was friendly. He spoke the words with a practiced military formality. Had he said only so much, Father Sandy Cairns today might not be among the missing.

Sandy's mind leaped. He saw why the earlier looters had been so recklessly bold in their action. He saw why landings on Sancian were occurring so frequently. There was more he could have learned had the Japanese not added what may have been a kindly-meant offer but one which served to plant a germ of doubt in Sandy's mind.

"You leave here immediately and I can put you ashore on the mainland anywhere you choose," the officer added, without changing the tone of his voice. "If you wait for another opportunity someone else may be in charge. Someone else may not treat you as well as I shall."

Even if that statement was well meant, it blew out the fuse in Father Cairns' line of logic. There were a hundred occasions in the past when the Japanese had revealed their desire to rid the island of its Americans. These Americans, looking at every action of the secret-loving Imperial Navy, had been a thorn in the Japanese side. When the Japanese officer made that offer of help, suspicions began to smolder in the priest's mind. Why this bending over backward, if America and Japan were at war? Why such sudden solicitude? In his heart the priest thought that the same old game was being played, but this time with a little more subtlety. To him, lacking anything confirmatory, it seemed like a ruse. He decided he wasn't going to be its victim. His duty was on Sancian Island. If a war was in progress the men on the mainland would have sent news to him long before. He would stay.

The decision caused the officer to depart peremptorily. A military man, that man.

Actually, on the mainland, a wiry young priest from Massachusetts, Father Joseph Lavin, was making desperate attempts to get news to Father Cairns. From his mission at Hoignan, Father Lavin had twice tried to make the crossing to Sancian, but both times the boatmen had shaken their heads and put about. They couldn't make it. The renewed Japanese blockade offshore was too hazardous. Another time, adverse winds broke up a plan to get a small sailboat across.

Father Cairns was smart enough to play a safety-first game. Not sure whether the Japanese officer had spoken truly or falsely, he cautiously decided that the sisters and their charges should go to the mainland to spend the Christmas season. There, no matter what happened, they'd be safe. If the news were not true, it would be an easy matter for them to come back. Secretly he made preparations for two boats to leave, with the sisters, girls and a few families.

The boats left for the mainland in the pitch-black midnight of December 15-16. The sea was still running a heavy swell after a storm that had already delayed the departure a day and a half. Father Cairns, standing barefoot on the beach, helped them shove off. It was the last time those people were to see him. The next morning one of the boats, stranded for repairs on a distant island opposite Sancian, saw a Japanese motor launch, barely visible, draw up to the water front before the Mission, delay for a time, then leave. In it, according to later information, was Father Cairns. That day he learned that for once the Japanese had spoken the truth. There was a war going on.

What happened to Father Cairns after that we wait to know. We dare not believe the worst of the tales told, yet we cannot believe the best. Some time after his departure, Japanese warships drew up and shelled the mission. Then a party came ashore and burned it to the ground. The Japanese said the guerrillas were using the empty mission as a barracks.

The disconsolate fisher folk now gaze upon the skeleton walls and scattered ashes. They fear that their pastor is dead, but hope that he is alive, and they wonder if he will come back and rebuild their church. Sandy Cairns, the missioner who watched the sea roll in, the sky grow dark and the night come on over Sancian, remains missing. If he really is dead somewhere at the bottom of the South China Sea, his spirit isn't the kind that an ocean can hold down. That spirit would be negotiating in celestial courts on new business for Sancian Island and its fisher folk.

8 . . . Tales from Kweilin

LATE IN 1942 I was called to Kweilin, leaving the listening post in the capable hands of Father Theodore Bauman, a Divine Word Father who had made his way to Chungking when the war started. I flew to Kweilin, where refugees and missioners were arriving from Kwangtung. They brought both glowing and amusing tales of Father O'Neill, the Pastor of Toishan. After talking to these people I jotted down many notes about him and his game of hide-and-seek with the Japanese military.

A man from Hunan arrived at the house in Kweilin for a visit. He was Father Lloyd Glass, acting bishop and general trouble-shooter for all the missioners of that province. His humorous stories of what he was going through kept us listening late into the night. Next day I wrote them down.

The two priests were as unlike as Rhode Island and Iowa where they were born, but they had taken the same road through life and met with the same problems. Each was a study, for each had met his problems in a distinctive and individual way.

Brought up on an Iowa farm, Lloyd Glass as a boy pitched wheat into the threshing machine, shocked oats and rode triumphant on top of wagons piled with timothy. Iowa milk and Iowa corn put 190 pounds of muscle and bone on him before he went to Columbia College, and it didn't take the football coach long to turn him into a roaring guard. Roaring was the word for Glass—he was always roaring with merriment and laughter. At the end of each football season he trained in the ring and wound up as C. C.'s champion heavyweight for 1931. Then, after completing his arts course, he astonished his classmates by entering the seminary at Maryknoll. He left his helmet and padded togs behind, but he took the boxing gloves along. He also took a racket, for he was an excellent tennis player, and this skill served him well later on.

Because of his overwhelming energy and good humor, together with his unusual understanding of human nature, Father Glass was singled out by his superiors as a natural trouble-shooter soon after he arrived in China. This was in 1937, the year Japan launched its war against Chiang Kai-shek's Republic. For example, in a certain city the local authorities were unfriendly and made trouble for the church. Father Glass went up there and called on the chief magistrate. He soon drew him into a discussion of sports. Next, he had him playing tennis at the mission. He let him win often enough so that the magistrate thought himself a big tennis player, and in a few weeks they were slapping each other on the back. The trouble disappeared.

On a December evening in 1941, everything seemed peaceful as Father Glass, his round of autumn visits completed, entered his home in Yungfu. But he had no sooner crossed the threshold than the young priest he had left in charge met him with a long face: "The Japanese have attacked us at Pearl Harbor," he said. Then he handed Father Glass a telegram from Msgr. Romaniello: PACK BAGS COME KWEILIN GO HUNAN IMMEDIATELY.

There was trouble in Hunan. The Japanese, whose occupation did not yet extend below Hankow on the Yangtze, had made several southward thrusts in anticipation of their campaign to link their forces in the north and south, cutting China in two. They had twice invaded the key rail city of Changsha; there the Italian missioners (Milan fathers) remained at their posts while the enemy came and went. This led to suspicion, resentment and accusations on the part of the Chinese authorities, who proceeded to intern the priests. These sent a message to Msgr. Romaniello asking that someone care for the missions in their absence.

Father Glass traveled several days by train, bus, truck and sampan to Siangtan, where he found Bishop Calzolari, with several priests and other Axis nationals. Guards told him the missioners had been accused of espionage, sabotage and other fifth column activities. It was said they possessed Japanese Friendship Badges, a wireless sending set and a small arsenal. The evidence had been forwarded to Loyang, the provincial capital. Here Father Glass found another Italian prelate, Bishop Lacchio, with his priests and some sisters.

Before many days the bouncing American missioner was hobnobbing with the authorities. Next, he generously offered to look over the evidence himself. The badges turned out to be baptismal certificates. The sending set was an outmoded radio, long out of order. The arsenal was a rusty old revolver without shells. Father Glass had a lot of fun with this. Although the hammer could hardly be forced back, he showed the round-eyed officials just how cowboys draw and shoot from the hip. The charges against the missioners were lifted, but the Chinese insisted on keeping all Axis nationals interned. Two of the Italian bishops asked Father Glass to be their Vicar Delegate in a territory as large as New England. Soon the churches and mission properties in the area were being managed by American priests under Father Glass.

This did not mean his job was done. Local rowdies would take over a mission here; looters would annoy a convent there. Father Glass hopped from one to the other, patching things up. A Hungarian bishop sent him an SOS: a Chinese commander had occupied the mission and orphan home and confiscated the ricefields that yielded the orphans' food. Father

Glass went, sized up the commander and invited him to a banquet. Previously he had ascertained that the bishop had succeeded in hiding a little red wine and apricot brandy. These Father Glass served to his military guest, along with a succession of rollicking stories. He also made a point of showing his American passport and of dwelling on the importance of the new Chinese-American alliance. Before the evening was over, the commander was toasting President Roosevelt, the Hungarian bishop and Father Glass. Next day he took his soldiers away.

Father Glass was acting bishop and general trouble-shooter for a year, at the end of which, as a result of his ingenuity and labor, many of the interned missioners were allowed to go back to their posts. Throughout the many privations which he suffered in carrying out this delicate and sometimes risky task, Father Glass never once lost his great sense of humor, attested by many of his letters to his bishop. "I've got to get some sisters here," he wrote from a station of the Luxemburg nuns, who had been taken away from the orphanage into concentration. "I'm not at my best washing diapers, you know."

On receiving instructions to return to Kweilin, he wrote: "I'll be glad to get home for a rest. Haven't killed anyone yet and I hope to keep my record clean. The sooner I leave the more hope there is." He wrote that one of the reinstated Italian bishops had said in a public address, "God sent Father Glass to help us," and in the letter to Msgr. Romaniello, who sent him, he added, "That steps you up into high places, Bishop."

After a few weeks' vacation, the Iowa battler was put to a new test, that of opening a mission in a town which had never had a priest. This is the most difficult job in the mission field. The town was Patpo, a coal-mining center among the abrupt rocky hills to the east of Kweilin. "A city," Father Glass wrote, "of 15,000, mostly Chinese, with three banks, a government hospital and cheap coal—but food scarcer than grass on the desert." He rented a mud-walled shop, quickly made friends with the local officials and was soon part of the town's life, visiting the sick, helping the poor and bringing to all the comforting words of Christianity.

Not that he didn't have his little troubles, "The boy Wu Yu is here with me," he wrote, "splashing whitewash here and there and tearing things up and down. . . . Between times, Wu Yu throws some grub together on the table. As a cook he is not a bad mason. A month here and I'll be able to digest boulders—or else I'll be lying under some, like McGinty. With Wu Yu as a cook, what I want for a curate is a man who likes rice, bean curd and peppers; and who if necessary can earn money crawling on his belly in a coal mine, for prices are getting higher and higher and higher."

While these troubles were buffeting the mission at Hunan, Father Francis O'Neill in the district of Toishan was not without some of his own. Added to the grief brought by the emissaries of the Rising Sun, in 1943 a drought and flood created in Toishan its worst famine of the century.

Father O'Neill's station was one of the most perilous in the mission field. Toishan (whence come 90 per cent of Chinese who migrate to America) is on a branch of the West River which forms the southern boundary of the Canton Delta. On the north bank were the Japanese, entrenched with pillboxes, machine guns, field guns and mortars. On the south bank, as firm as a pillbox in his determination to carry on the church and relief work, was Father O'Neill.

His parishioners, who could not very well move away, were inmates of the mission's small hospital, and orphans. He had a particular way with children: eldest in his family, he had helped raise five little brothers and sisters. Even after he grew up his favorite song was "Toyland, Joyland, Dear-Little-Girl-and-Boy-Land"—and many is the time he sang this ditty for a hundred or more doll-faced Chinese tots, whose eyes grew round as he did a sort of Irish jig to the tune.

Toishan was twice invaded by the Japanese before Pearl Harbor, and on each occasion Father O'Neill managed to send the children and sick people away to safety in the hills. But because he was a fighter as well as a singer and because he was a director who always wanted to be on the spot, helping others and working himself to exhaustion, he remained in the deserted city to watch his mission. The first time looters came to the gate he marched out to meet them like a Marine and told them to stay out. They did. But a second time, weeks later, a Japanese detail clattered up with bayonets fixed, beat him and looted the hospital—while other soldiers, breaking into stores and homes, killed a hundred and eighty men, women and children. In a sportive mood, the soldiers then threw a corpse under the mission windows.

But Father O'Neill was not discouraged. He wangled a pass from the Japanese commander and was able to bring food to a small colony of lepers which he ran on the city's outskirts. In those days, before war with the United States, the Japanese sometimes treated Americans with courtesy and friendliness. A soldier came in one day as Father O'Neill was brewing coffee and politely asked for a cup. The priest gave it to him, remarking that he was sorry there was no sugar. The following day the grateful ruffian came around with a bag of sugar from the general loot.

Another time, a group came around that weren't so courteous or obliging, and Father O'Neill, who had heard they were requisitioning vehicles, was prepared for them. When the detail appeared to demand his priceless motorcycle, he shrugged resignedly and pointed to the shed where it was kept. The tank was empty, but the soldiers filled it with gas—then pushed the bike up and down the street for an hour. It wouldn't run. Nothing would make it so much as sputter, and they finally left it at the mission gate, forgetting in their rage to empty the tank of the precious fuel they had supplied. "Toyland, Joyland . . ." whistled Father O'Neill through his teeth after they had gone, as he quietly restored a vital little gadget he had removed from the motor.

Almost every city in that part of Kwangtung province had been bombed many times, but Toishan had the dragon's share of punishment over a period of five years. If it wasn't bullets whining in the streets or looters rapping on the mission gate, it was artillery shells and air bombs that made the thick walls rock. Father O'Neill's little hospital overflowed into his home during some of the air raids, and his great energy was taxed to the limit. During one two-hour raid he saw a wall crumble across the street, trapping a child. He dashed over, dug the victim free and started to run for it with the child in his arms; he had not gone twenty steps before he was knocked down by the concussion of a bomb that dug a crater on the spot from which he had rescued the child. A crowd witnessed this action, and Father O'Neill was presented with a testimonial banner by the city. Whenever a foreigner is given a testimonial banner in China, he as good as owns the town.

But Toishan was no cinch to own, or even to live in, after Pearl Harbor and the fall of near-by Hongkong. Stepped-up Japanese aggression sent an enormous wave of refugees into the city and its surrounding villages; at the same time, virtually all supplies were cut off. With funds from the American Advisory Committee of United China Relief, Father O'Neill hired an old temple under whose winglike eaves he set up a circle of caldrons of boiling gruel, rice and beans. Here each noon a thousand old people, women and children gathered in queues waiting to be fed. He doled out the rations personally; he would have fed more, but food was scarce and he gave meal tickets only in cases of the direst need. Consumption was prevalent among adults, and most of the children had pinched faces, bloated bellies and bony limbs.

Then in 1943 both the spring and fall crops failed, and starvation gripped Toishan in earnest. Many an evening as he went home from the temple, half-blind with fatigue, Father O'Neill saw in the roadside shadows the body of some woman or child who had just died of hunger. As the famine grew worse and more and more people died, the priest added grave-digging to his many self-imposed labors.

He was now running a mission, a hospital (in which he acted as an anesthetist), an orphanage, a leper asylum—doing everything himself, neglecting to eat and to sleep. The bishop heard that his health was in danger and sent a priest to spell him. The assistant reported that each afternoon about five Father O'Neill would come into the mission, find himself a chair and just sit in it for a few minutes, his eyes glassy with fatigue, his lips apart. Then he would eat a small bowl of rice, which was practically all his food for the day, and rest a little more before going out to dig another grave or attend to the sick refugees in the hospital. When he was nagged into taking a vacation, he merely went to the big leper colony down the river and worked harder than ever.

That year fifty-two hundred people starved in Toishan, and every one of them took away a little bit of the song from the heart of Francis O'Neill. One day he failed to rise from his regular five o'clock fadeout. The little fighter from Rhode Island had fought his campaign: he was put in his own hospital suffering from tuberculosis.

9 . . . The Unpredictable

THE SUMMER OF 1943 BROUGHT to our Chungking listening post news that was bright and news that was tragic. Bishop Adolph Paschang, Maryknoll Bishop of Kongmoon, and Father Anthony Paulhus, Rector of the Kongmoon Seminary, had managed their escape from internment at Macao; American Franciscan Fathers arrived in Chungking, chased by the Japanese, and the much-bombed Father Sprinkle nearly lost his life when the Japanese destroyed the Wuchow mission.

At the outbreak of war, Bishop Paschang, three priests and two Maryknoll Sisters were arrested and taken off to the Portuguese colony of Macao for internment. Although Japanese sentries guarded the city, Father Smith and Father North had escaped safely. Bishop Paschang and Father Paulhus were encouraged by their success and planned to get away themselves. Late at night the two clergymen, dressed in Chinese clothes, quietly stole from their house and made their way to the water front. Here three Chinese were waiting with a small boat. The bishop and priest climbed aboard, and the boatmen silently dipped their oars, pushing away from shore.

They got out through the harbor unchallenged and by daybreak were pulling up the coast to land in Free China. A Japanese patrol boat spied the unidentified sampan creeping along the shore and bore down on it. The three Chinese and two clergymen jumped ashore and dropped behind a dike. The Chinese were guerrillas and they had three Belgian-made machine guns. Using the dike as a barricade, they would fire a spurt from the machine gun, then run behind the wall a few yards and fire another, to give the impression they were there in force. In the dim light of dawn the Japanese were puzzled and feared a trap. After firing many rounds against the thick wall, the Japanese patrol boat withdrew.

When all was quiet, the guerrilla soldiers led the bishop and Father Paulhus up into the hills, where they joined a large band of their comrades. The guerrillas fed the missioners, cared for them and led them back into Free China, where they resumed their mission tasks for the Chinese.

Just as this news was coming in, a group of American Franciscan Fathers arrived in Chungking. Father Cletus Hughes and Father Blaise Scannell were the first to arrive. They had been caught between the firing lines several times and for seventeen days had been forced to live on soybeans and sleep in the fields, during their journey of almost seven hundred miles over rough terrain.

Father Scannell told us that when the Japanese invaded their mission at Shasi, Hupeh, they were forced to live in small country mission stations. They hoped to get back to their own mission if the Japanese retreated. Instead, the enemy advanced west and forced them to flee farther into the interior. They crossed the mountains into Western Hupeh and finally reached the Belgian Franciscans in Ichang. But the Japanese were pushing close, so they came to Chungking.

One of their men, Father Rock, was caught by the Japanese, and nothing has been heard from him since.

Father Scannell went to the radio station with me to listen to the story of Father Sprinkle, which had just come in, being broadcast to America.

Father Sprinkle had been in China seven years and had survived some of the worst Japanese bombings. He was known to fellow missioners as The Unpredictable because of his unorthodox methods, his indefatigable energy and his way of riding a broken-down motorbike which another priest had thrown on the junk heap three years before. This mechanical marvel is still in service. Father Sprinkle runs beside it to start the motor, reaches down to the gear housing to shift because the shift lever is gone, pulls another wire to open up the gas, and jumps on. He rides off so fast that any priest seeing him start out is prepared for a funeral. No one dares to follow him through the narrow country paths; those who have to ride out with him always insist on going in front.

A couple of years earlier, a bomb landed in the mission yard near the shack in which he kept his treasured Lizzie. After the dust had settled, Father Sprinkle worked feverishly, digging the bike out of the collapsed garage. After toggling her up with a few more wires, he made her go again. Then he wired a St. Christopher medal to the frame—and what a load he put on the poor Saint's shoulders! Incidentally, amid the shrapnel he found a piece engraved "Cleveland, Ohio." He uses it as a paperweight—"my gift from the old Buckeye State."

After that near miss, Father Sprinkle decided to beat it out into the country during air raids. On one of these trips, as he sped down a winding, dusty path, he came to a ditch spanned only by a narrow plank. With customary recklessness, he gave Lizzie the gas—but this time it happened. Both landed in mud and water six feet below. Though he denies it, fellow priests say he lectured St. Christopher next day: "I'll give you one more chance. But let me down again, and off my bike you go!"

Chinese are getting used to mechanical contraptions by now, but in those days a motorcycle was regarded as one of the seven wonders of the world. When villagers heard one coming they would run as fast as they could in the opposite direction, or duck behind the big trunk of a banyan tree, or race into whatever they used for an air-raid shelter. Then they would peer out cautiously to determine if it was a Japanese

plane or merely the Shen Fu (Spiritual Father) coming their
way again.

As soon as the bike stood still, with its motor quiet, a crowd
of men and women and children would gather around it
reverently and offer whispered guesses as to what devil made
it go. Soon the youngsters would gain courage and start tinkering. The horn, the most obvious thing to operate, would get a
thorough workout. One lad would honk it unmercifully, scar-
ing chickens and livestock. His buddy wouldn't believe it made
all that din until he himself took a turn at squeezing the rubber
bulb. Then one of the grownups would want to make sure, and
so on down the line, until everybody was satisfied. The more
daring ones would then test the lights and spark plugs and
jerk a few wires, crying out "Ai-yah!" when they touched the
hot cylinder flanges. And while this was going on, some chap
who had visited the city near by would deliver a windy, inac-
curate lecture on the secrets of machinery.

These little motorbikes were invaluable for sick calls and
other mission emergencies, but they had to be guarded like
diamonds from curious meddlers, particularly children. This
curiosity is utterly uninhibited, and no ordinary barrier will
prevent them from penetrating into a compound or building
if there is something there that interests them.

A small boy and his sister appeared one day at the side of
Father James Gilloegly of Scranton, a newcomer to Father
Sprinkle's mission, demanding that he take them each for a
ride on his motorbike. He said he had work to do, but they
followed him into his study, chirping, "Work later, work later,"
and tugging at the wide sleeves of his Chinese jacket, until he
told the ten-year-old girl, "Your mother might need you. You
ought to go home."

She replied, "Don't want to," like little girls the world over.

"Oh, so that's it," smiled Father Gilloegly and turned to
her brother, who had found the office alarm clock and was

trying to make it ring. "You go and tell your father and mother," said the priest, "that Bright Nature does not wish to return home." Immediately brother lost all interest in the alarm clock. Both children stared, and Bright Nature insisted desperately that she had never said such a thing. When the puzzled priest started to repeat his seemingly simple adjuration, she placed a hand over his mouth, looked solemnly into his eyes and shook her head.

At supper Father Gilloegly, still perplexed, told his colleagues what had happened and a roar of laughter went up around the table. "Bright Nature does not wish to return home," echoed Father Sprinkle, as the laughter quieted down. "You don't know what that means around here? I am indeed surprised at you, Father Gilloegly. Why, you proposed to her!"

After the tempo of the Pacific war speeded up and Japan began hitting hard at the American bases in southern and western China, Father Sprinkle and his fellow missioners in Wuchow had some trying times. In the middle of March, 1943, a formation of twenty-eight bombers came over and blasted the city as well as the field across the river. It was the first big raid in many months, and Father Sprinkle and Father James Smith—who escaped from internment at Macao and later became my assistant at Chungking—stood fascinated on the mission porch instead of taking cover in the underground shelter.

The planes came in at a slanting dive, and with hellish noise aimed at the roofs. The bays opened right over the priests' heads, and as the death load came tumbling out, they fell flat on the ground. The sizzling, frying sound of bombs falling at them gave them just a second to think, "The end is near." With a deafening explosion the house rocked and swayed. The glass in the windows crashed, window frames and doors were splintered into kindling wood and went flying in every direction. Chairs and tables were hurled against the walls and heavy wardrobes crashed to the floor. Then tiles, bricks and dirt rained down. Incendiaries dropped on the mission's flat tile roof. Other incendiaries started eating into the debris of wrecked houses all around the mission, and fire crackling through the dry wood on all sides struck more terror into their hearts. The convent was two blocks away, and there was only one alley of escape. Father Sprinkle and Father Smith wondered if the sisters were cut off by fire. They could not leave their own fire-ringed mission now. (They later learned the sisters were so busy putting out the incendiary bombs in the courtyard that they did not think of the trap of blazing homes around them.) Across the street from the mission house was a carpenter shop, fire spouting from every door and window. Black smoke was spiraling toward the sky and crackling fires were leaping up on the other three sides of the mission. Before the hum of the planes was out of hearing, bells and whistles filled the air as fire-fighting units rushed through the streets.

One of the buildings on the mission grounds had been blasted open by a bomb. Flush against it was a house four stories high. A demolition bomb blew out its foundation, and it pancaked. The northeast wind was crowding and licking flames the other way, and the missioners could get close enough to fight the approaching fire. People under the rubble were screaming for help. Father Smith and Father Sprinkle had mobilized the cook, the house boy and teachers, and all poured water into the creeping flames. One teacher somehow got out through the flames to call a fire-fighting unit and a hose into that area.

The priests and the fire squad ran back and forth with buckets between the emergency tank and the fire. Their backs ached, their hands became blistered and burned, their legs nearly buckled with fatigue, but they blocked the flames from the pile of timbers that covered screaming people. The priests shouted at all who came near to dig out the buried victims while they poured on water. Stretcher bearers came and worked frantically, while some citizens stood around in a daze until Father Sprinkle yelled at them, "Dig, dig, dig!"

Some of the helpers fainted as men, women and children were dragged out of the pile, many with part of a limb blown off and the bone sticking out. Those who were dying were brought to the fire-fighting fathers. One of these would stop long enough to give a few sentences of instruction, then he would dip his hand in the fire pail and dash water on the victim's head in baptism.

All afternoon the fathers strained and fought against the fire to save the mission.

As night drew near, the missioners knew they had won against the flames. Then they joined the rescue squads to dig through the water and rubble. Now and then they dug to a person still living; now and then they could save a soul where they caught a person turning the last corner.

Going down through the streets that night, they passed smoking ruins. They saw wailing women sitting on piles of rubble that once were homes. They found two little children crying their eyes out for Ahmah, a mother that perhaps would never come back. They saw mangled corpses that rescue squads had left in order to look for wounded. They saw people digging in what had been the homes of the poor for a kettle, a pot or a pan in which to cook their morning rice. As they went home to sleep before the next day's work, the missioners estimated that the raid had created about two thousand homeless wanderers. The mission aided the families that had lost everything. Police registered those whose homes were destroyed and gave each family a certificate. Then came the rice dole line for those who were homeless; the street to the mission was crowded with victims presenting their certificates.

After the raid Father Sprinkle found that the buttons of his Chinese coat had been torn off by a bomb explosion. One

lens in Father Smith's spectacles was shattered. Father Sprinkle is convinced that Providence and St. Christopher watched
over him in a special way. He kept his Saint Christopher
medal on his wired-up motorbike and went on tearing between
rice paddies and over planks across ditches, to visit his flock
in the village.

A later raid that same year destroyed the three-story, stone-
walled mission building, but not Father Sprinkle or his bike
where the patient St. Christopher kept vigil. Shortly after
breakfast one day in October, 1943, an unusually large swarm
of Japanese bombers came droning over the city, and the mission's air-raid shelter was quickly packed. But Father Sprinkle
was nowhere to be found. "He is probably upstairs watching
the whole thing," Father Reilly, with a worried shake of his
head, told a visitor, Father Francis Lynch of Pittsfield, Mass.
They called out but there was no answer. The enemy planes
were close now, and the first bombs were exploding. The
priests sought cover, and, knowing the shelter was full, they
went to the little chapel in the basement.

Here, praying in the dim light of flickering votive tapers,
were three nuns and eleven children. In the front pew knelt
Sister Agnes Virginia Higgins, of Nebraska, superior of the
convent. Near by was Sister Henrietta Marie Cunningham of
Massachusetts, who had lived through days of terror in Japanese-occupied Hongkong. In the rear Sister Mary Chanel
knelt, quietly telling her beads and inspiring calm in the boys
and girls about her. Suddenly Sister Mary rose and motioned
her pupils to follow. She led them up to the pews near the
altar, and this move saved their lives.

A stick of bombs fell across the mission, and for seconds
all life was suspended in the indescribable vacuum of destruction. When people were able to breathe and move again and
the choking cloud of lime dust had thinned so they could see,

they found that, unbelievably, they had survived in the midst of complete ruin.

No one in the chapel was so much as scratched—although the rear pews, from which Sister Mary Chanel had removed her children, was piled head-high with fallen masonry. Everybody in the shelter was accounted for. Only Father Sprinkle was missing.

The entire structure above ground had crumbled into mounds of smoking timbers, shattered bricks, crushed red tiles. As Father Reilly dashed from one pile of ruins to another, searching for a trace of Father Sprinkle, he heard a weak but familiar voice: "Help, I'm over here. Hurry."

The Unpredictable was invisible under a mass of twisted metal and tortured masonry. It took them an hour to dig him out. Two third-floor beams had descended with him and pinned down his chest and abdomen. One eye was shut, and his clothing was clotted with blood. At the Stout Memorial Hospital outside the town, Dr. Wallace found that the priest's jaw and right hip were fractured. He was flat on his back for three months, his body in a cast. As soon as he heard that Lizzie had been found, more or less intact as usual, he ordered St. Christopher taken off and wired to his bed.

II . . . Betrayal in the North

1 . . . The City of Orchids

WHILE THE SNOWS MELTED in the spring of 1944, trouble was brewing in China's northwest. Bishop Buddenbrock, Superior of the Divine Word Fathers in Lanchow, capital of Kansu province, sent me letters that read like an SOS. He begged me to come. There was danger that his dispensaries and schools would be forced to close, and he was also having financial troubles. Most of his missioners happened to be German nationals, and he felt that as an American I might help them iron out their difficulties. Some of them had been exiled from neighboring Sinkiang by Soviet police, and the bishop intimated that they had much to tell me which could not safely be sent through the mails.

Then William Bentz, Swedish representative for the International Red Cross, returned from Lanchow, bringing me a letter from one of the exiled missioners. It told of unbelievable torture and persecution suffered by the priests in Sinkiang. The writer wanted me to go to Lanchow and get their reports and pass them on to the Divine Word American Mission headquarters at Techny, Illinois.

Stanley Smith, British Embassy press attaché and Ministry of Information director in Chungking, had just made a trip to Lanchow. On his return he invited me to dinner and told enthralling tales of political troubles, intrigue and espionage in the frontier city. Sitting around the fireplace piled high with Chungking's smoky soft coal, he told me among other things

79

of a man named Hunter, whose startling story had never been written.

"Go to Lanchow," he urged. "You'll hear most unusual stories, meet remarkable men and sense the mysterious atmosphere of this crossroads city where Europe and Asia mingle."

It was difficult for anyone to go to Lanchow. Because I was a member of the American, the Catholic and the International Relief Committees, which sent funds regularly to Lanchow, I was able to obtain a visa after much negotiation to inspect the relief work there, and within two weeks I had boarded a Douglas plane heading north.

We were nearing the end of our three-and-a-half-hour trip when the clouds suddenly broke and I had my first view of this key region of China's northwest. The plane was leaping over mountains two miles high. The ride was bumpy, for it was past eleven o'clock and hot currents of air were rising into the cold. The sand was silver white on the plains below, but the gray loess soil was terraced in crazy-quilt patterns on the sides of the mountains where wheat is grown. Because Kansu is flanked on the north by the Great Gobi Desert and on the west by the Little Gobi, the dry eroded country over which we were flying received only ten to twelve inches of rainfall a year. While the tall mountains reach up to steal the mists and gentle rains from the clouds, the lowlands suffered an endless drought.

The plane allowed us a good view of Lanchow as it circled to land. My first glimpse of the northwest metropolis was a little disappointing. From the air it seemed more like a sprawling town than a city, with its rambling low buildings hedged in by walls, and crooked roads spreading over the plain. The clusters of boxlike houses are built with walls of gray adobe soil. The flat roofs are covered with desert sand dropped by the wind. These homes look much like the adobe houses of the Indians in Arizona or New Mexico. Around the city are high walls with lookout towers, and far in the north can be seen the Great Wall of China, looping down as extra protection for the fabled City of Orchids, gateway to Central Asia. Here on the upper reaches of the Hoang-Ho, where high mountains squeeze the water into a narrow hurrying stream, travelers, nomads, or perhaps just a flower lover found orchids in profusion. And so, far back in time, some dreamer called the place Lanchow (or Kaolan), which in English means "The Bank of Orchids."

I stepped out of the plane into a cool, dry climate which gives a dash of red to the cheeks of the people. Many of the tall, big-framed men look not unlike American Indians. There are, as I learned later, many things that mark Lanchow as a frontier city and remind one of the border towns of our own Southwest in the last century, when immigrants, prospectors, gold-seekers, cowboys and Indians made life gay and interesting.

In the years which saw the dawn of Christianity, only Mongolians and Tibetans peopled the land around Lanchow. The high South Mountains of Kansu formed a loose dividing line for the Tibetans to the south and the Mongolians to the north. Invading armies of these two peoples swept in periodically and fought to control the Lanchow plain. Outside the city is the tomb of the Great Khan, the Mongol warrior whose conquests were the vastest the world has ever known.

Chinese migrated to the province in later centuries. Famines uprooted them from the cities and farmlands of Honan and they moved west. The Emperor at Peking banished many political offenders to Kansu. Eventually, by dint of superiority in numbers, the Chinese gained control and ruled the province.

Then out of the west in Central Asia came the fiercest fighters of them all, the Turki Moslems, sword-swinging fanat-

ics who massacred in the name of Allah. There are only thirty
thousand in Kansu today, but they ruled the province until the
last decade. The Moslems resent the transfer of control to
Chungking, and are constantly on the verge of revolt. General
Pai Ts'ung Hsi, the Mohammedan general from Kwangsi, is
periodically sent by Chiang Kai-shek to negotiate with the
Moslems in the Lanchow area, in order to keep them tied to
the Central Government. Moslems do not like the Chinese,
and they hate the Communists and disdain the Tibetans and
Mongolians.

Communist armies were the latest to sweep into the Lanchow plain. Ten years ago, when Chu Teh and his Red troops
were pushed out of Kiangsi province in the south, they
marched up through Kansu on their way to Sinkiang. In the
corridor northwest of Lanchow, the Communists were defeated by Mohammedan General Ma and retreated back across
Lanchow to Yenan, in Shensi province, where they reorganized
and set up their present headquarters.

It is the result of all these movements and counter-move-
ments that one sees in the streets of Lanchow. Trucks and cars
speed up and down the streets beside camels, mules and oxen.
Smart young people in western dress pass Mongolians and
Tibetans in the same decorative dress their ancestors wore centuries ago.

I found myself rubbing shoulders with the tall-hatted
Tibetan, the olive-skinned, bearded Turki Moslem, the pure
Old Mongolian, many types of Chinese, and the Marxist and
Czarist Russian. The Mongol type predominated. I saw shop
signs in Chinese, in Russian, in Turki and a few in Tibetan
and in English.

There are braying donkeys with heavy loads strapped to
their backs, long-haired camels chewing their cuds, and herds
of yaks, with hair hanging like silky tresses, being driven in
from the mountains for slaughter. Stout mules hitched in line

to high-wheeled carts haul salt, coal and other freight along
the rutted byroad that runs parallel to the auto route. Winds
from the desert have brought a dust carpet to the land. As your
shoes come down in the velvety powdered clay, dust fluffs out
on all sides. On the street we met a barber with a portable
tonsorial parlor on a shoulder pole, walking through the market
looking for trade. On one end of his pole is a stool for a barber's chair, with drawers full of clippers, razors, shears, combs
and brushes—and tools for digging the wax out of the client's
ears. The other end of the pole carries a stove, hot water and
towels. Whenever a customer calls, on a street corner, in a shop
or in the market-place, he sets up and goes to work.

In the kaleidoscope of curiosities along the streets there
was one high-wheeled cart that particularly caught my eye.
On the cart was a blown-up cowhide that made you wonder if
the cow had jumped out of its skin. Skinners start from the
head and skin the hide off as we pull a sweater over our heads.
The feet and neck are then tied up and the skin is used as a
tank car to transport all sorts of things. This particular cowskin
was filled with vegetable oil, and when buyers came up with
their jugs, the string on one leg was loosened for the oil to run
out of the skin. Up river the people fill these cowhides with
wheat, tie them together, and with a few boards on top for
a raft, float the wheat cargo down to Lanchow.

The news of D-day in Europe broke shortly after my arrival. Everybody was excitedly fingering the columns of curv-
ing characters that make up the flimsy, bamboo-paper
Lanchow dailies. Shopkeepers, sidewalk vendors, officials, all
cheered the long-awaited invasion and speculated on the approaching end of the war in Europe. When I went to the China
Inland Mission to call on our consul, Harry E. Stephens, the
mission treasurer met me at the door and we discussed the
good news. But when I tried to pump him a little on the situa-

tion in Lanchow, he said, "We don't talk about that sort of thing here. You never know who you are talking to—and it's important for us to keep clear of trouble."

People talked of politics only in whispers in this city where Mongol, Tibetan, Chinese, Moslem and Communist interests have clashed so many times in the past. Now belligerent Moslems who had ruled the country until recently were restive; temporarily silenced Russophiles, who wanted to see here a bridgehead from Russia into China, watched and planned, biding their time; Chu Teh's Chinese Communists, with headquarters in neighboring Yenan, abetted the Russophiles' intrigues; while the worried Central Government, knowing that China's security lies in control of the turbulent northwest, was busy strengthening its hand.

Our talk was interrupted by the arrival of A. M. Ledovsky, consul for the U.S.S.R. and formerly of the Soviet Embassy in Chungking. He came with a Russian assistant, in a car driven by a Russian chauffeur. It was amusing to observe that there seemed to be a change of role in Lanchow, for the "rich American capitalist" lived quite simply, while the "poor Russian Communist," I found, occupied a spacious home and offices and was served by a large staff.

I was a little surprised when Ledovsky invited me to his home to dinner. Perhaps he wanted to find out what I was doing in this hotbed of conflicting interests. With us at the table were three other Russians—members of his staff, the consul said. They asked a lot of questions, trying to draw me out. When they found it couldn't be done, the chat was light and pleasant. The consul proposed a toast to President Roosevelt, which we drank. In return I proposed drinking a toast to the United Nations. Perhaps he expected me to toast Stalin, or at least wondered if I would.

After dinner came dull Russian movies, but the consul sat beside me and we had an interesting conversation. In answer

to my question about religion in Russia, he told me he was
an atheist, though his mother was a devout believer. He said
that during the war the Communists were pleased with the
co-operation of the Russian Church, and as a result were giving
religion more freedom, though, he added reassuringly, people
always had the right to believe and practice if they wanted to.

During the movie he remarked that I was staying with
the Divine Word Fathers and asked, "Why do the Chinese
officials here treat those enemy nationals better than they treat
us Russians?"

I gave a noncommittal answer. It seemed to me that anyone old enough to know the time of day could grasp the fact
that the Chinese desperately feared the Russian machine's influence in the Lanchow area, whereas they had nothing to
fear from the German missioners. At the end of a pleasant
evening, the chauffeur escorted me to the Divine Word Mission in a car full of Russians.

The missioners with whom I was staying had been apprehensive of the closing of their dispensaries and schools. They
had always enjoyed friendly relations with the government,
but some local doctors and teachers, for reasons of their own,
were agitating against them as enemy nationals and pressing
the government to restrict their activities. As an American and
friendly national I went to visit the officials with Father Sange,
delegate of the bishop. We were assured that the missioners'
fears were exaggerated. The schools and dispensaries would
be permitted to continue unmolested.

The missioners' library and museum, their school of paint-
ing and music, and their interest in research, gained a high
place for them in Lanchow. The cathedral is the city's outstanding structure. It is built in old Chinese temple style;
corners of the roof and towers curve out and up like eagle
wings hovering over the town. On the big feasts there are as

many pagans and non-Catholic officials present in the cathedral as there are Catholics. They come to watch the ceremonies and procession and listen to the superb choir of Seminarians.

The high point of interest is a treasure room in the museum. It is full of burial urns, stone knives and axes used by people who lived here five thousand years ago. From this soil full of secrets, the story of these people was discovered in 1923 by Dr. Anderson of Sweden and an archaeological research party that excavated plateau graves in the P'o River Valley.

Prehistoric man roamed over this region before the use of metals was known. He could not write, but he could fashion clay into vessels, and in his love of art he drew designs of beauty on the clay he molded and baked into urns. When one of these ancient dwellers died his remains were carried to a terrace or plateau on the hills. With him in the grave they placed burial urns, and often in the urns were his stone ax and knife—the furniture of his time.

To you and me the ceramic designs baked into these urns mean little except as things of beauty. But to the anthropologists and archaeologists they are a book. Dr. Anderson says the urns are of the period 3500-3000 B.C. The designs on the pottery are the same as those on pottery found in the Near East, Mesopotamia and Greece, and cause the archaeologists to conjecture that men migrated here across Central Asia more than five thousand years ago.

After Dr. Anderson left, the missioners in the district went to work with the local people. They worked like ants in the P'o Valley and in other spots of the province and unearthed two hundred or more of these precious relics. The collection intrigued me, for it was at once a book of history and a work of art. I wondered about the men whose fingers fashioned this pottery so long ago. I wondered how they talked, what their religion might have been, what they thought of life and death.

At the mission one day we had an unusual guest. He was a Living Buddha from the Tibetan borderland monastery at Kumbum, Tsinghai. The former ruling Buddha of Kumbum, who died before him, is supposed to have become incarnate again in this man. This Living Buddha with his retinue stayed at the Catholic Mission in Lanchow on his way to Chungking to treat with the Central Government. I talked with him through an interpreter who spoke Chinese, since the Living Buddha spoke only Tibetan. When a Buddha dies, the lamas or monks go on a long search for a child who is his reincarnation. This child is brought to the lamasery to grow up and become the ruler of the region.

A curious friendship exists between the missionaries and the lamas. Catholic missioners passing in the vicinity of Kumbum lamasery stay with the lamas, and the lamas when in Lanchow put up at the mission. A few years ago the Panchen Lama was the guest of Bishop Buddenbrock and received his visitors in Lanchow at the mission.

From the Living Buddha of Kumbum I received a souvenir. It was a good luck charm, an amulet which Tibetans wear around the neck. It contained magic pills, a Buddhist saint's whiskers, and two little idols, together with other mystic prayers and charms. During our visit, the Living Buddha told me much about the prayers, beliefs and ceremonies of their cult. The amulet is now in our mission museum at Maryknoll on the Hudson.

2 . . . Oil and Espionage

ACROSS THE LONG IRON BRIDGE, which looks like an old-fashioned railroad span, at the edge of Lanchow is the famous Gateway to Central Asia. This beautiful stone portal with its three circular arches and winglike Chinese coping was partly demolished a few years ago, when the ancient caravan trail was widened into an auto road.

I went out to see the Gateway one day with some of my friends from the Divine Word Mission. As we chatted, a procession of trucks loaded with oil drums went by; they had come seven hundred miles from the west, from the Yumen fields near the Sinkiang border. The wells at Yumen, sunk in 1939, were China's first oil venture. They produce more than they can refine, for they lack equipment. They refine more than they can transport, for they lack facilities.

Looking at the trucks, I said Sinkiang was where I wanted to go, and my companions threw up their hands in caution: "If you do go, don't go alone. We would probably never hear of you again!"

I recalled then how some days earlier in Lanchow I had met a Chinese truck-driver I knew. He had just returned from Sinkiang, and I asked him to tell me about conditions there. He shook his head. "The secret police," he whispered, then drew his hand across his throat in an unmistakable gesture. I thought also of another friend, a Chinese banker who had returned to Chungking after vainly trying for eight months to establish a branch of his house in Sinkiang. He said, "The place is a nest of spies and hums with secret police. There are Communist party spies, Kuomintang spies, and spies of the provincial government."

Sinkiang, which is more than twice as large as France, is more nearly autonomous than any other Chinese province—even more so than Yunnan on the Burma border. Chungking will not grant a foreigner an entrance visa without an O.K. from Tihwa, or Urumchi, as the capital is variously known. No American citizens live there, yet it is significant that in 1943 Washington sent a consul, Howard Smith, to Tihwa. This was done partly in order to give face to China by recognizing its dominion over the province, and partly because Washington realizes that whoever controls Sinkiang in the future will control the swing of an enormous amount of trade one way or the other—to the United States or to Russia.

The history and strategic location of this remote nation in the heart of Asia is such that it is more and more often referred to as the Poland of the East. It is of vital importance to Russia, which it borders. Britain keeps an eye on its constant clashes and revolts, for it touches Tibet and Kashmir and casts a shadow over India. And as for China, she knows that in her struggle against Communism, Sinkiang is her Achilles' heel.

West from the Gateway at Lanchow stretches an eight-hundred-mile valley known as the Kansu Corridor. This corridor, which is at most only fifty miles wide, is formed by massive mountains on the south and by the equally rugged Northern Mountains on the edge of the Gobi Desert. It is the sole direct land route between China and Central Asia.

It is the most vital stretch of the historic Silk Route. Down this corridor came Marco Polo and other European explorers as the centuries rolled by. Turki Moslems swept down it to settle or control regions of western China. Chinese armies have rolled up it for conquest, fled down it in defeat. The shadows of endless caravans have darkened its sands—traders have

traveled it from east to west and west to east since earliest
history. Pack mules, horses, twin-humped camels have plodded
over the rough path with hides, wool, raisins or dried fruits
for China, and have trudged back with tea, silk, jade and
other merchandise for the West.

Early in this century, before the disintegration of the
Chinese Empire, the country at the western end of the Kansu
funnel was known as Chinese or East Turkestan; it was a
colony of the emperor, who formerly claimed also Outer Mongolia, Tibet, Burma and Indo-China in the colonial empire.
Then it became known as Sinkiang, the eighteenth province of
united Republican China; but Chiang Kai-shek's success in
bringing it under the wing of the Central Government has been
limited.

Chinese make up only 5 to 10 per cent of Sinkiang's three
and a half million inhabitants. Eastern Turks, who are Moslems, represent 75 per cent, and the balance consists of a dozen
other races, all with differences of language, character and
creed. The official language is Turki, with its varying dialects,
but Chinese, Mongolian, Russian, Kirgiz and other tongues
are spoken. The province is in constant turmoil—the people
are resigned to expecting a Moslem uprising regularly every
few years.

In the last half-century the Chinese government has attempted three separate—and abortive—settlement programs in
Sinkiang. The sands of the Kansu Corridor are speckled with
the chalky skulls of would-be Chinese settlers, as our own
southwestern deserts are dotted with the skulls of cattle. Recently the Chungking government worked out a new settlement program to aid victims of flood and famine in Honan
province. Under this plan, families are transported free of
charge to the fertile lands around Tihwa. Four Chinese acres,
or more, are allowed for each person in a family. The home-
steaders are fed free for six months and given farm implements,

seed, and beasts to work the land. The animals may be used three years before payment is demanded. Even lumber and other home-building materials are furnished gratis. But in spite of all this encouragement, only 7000 persons migrated to Sinkiang in 1943. The 1944 total, up to June, was 2300—against the 100,000 that Chiang Kai-shek had hoped for. There was some talk of sending 25,000 of his Youth Corps to Sinkiang but the plan was dropped.

The Chinese for the most part have looked on Sinkiang as a colony. They have gone there to gain wealth, then returned to the homeland. And vast wealth there is, though most of it is still to be developed.

The statement that Sinkiang is twice as large as France (or three times the size of Texas) may be misleading. Deserts and barren mountain ranges render two-thirds of it useless, or at least uninhabitable. Yet there are large fertile valleys, like those of Tihwa and Ili, still sparsely settled. Ten million sheep and a million and a half cattle graze on grassy high-lands, representing a vast trade in wool and hides. There are great untapped coal deposits almost everywhere. There is gold. And there is black gold—petroleum.

The only oil fields of commercial possibility discovered in China were found in the northwest. While I was in Lanchow a Mitchell bomber landed with a group of American officers who told me they were on their way to the new artesian fields at Yumen, several hundred miles up the Kansu Corridor; they were to check on the capacity of the output, which they said was "abundant." The Chinese say that since the wells were sunk there in 1939, taking that year as a base, the output for 1943 was 38,000 per cent. These wells were hastily put into operation, with the assistance of four American experts, when China's foreign oil supply was cut off by the war. While oil is plentiful, the refining facilities are primitive and makeshift, and the Japanese blockade has prevented bringing in up-to-date machinery.

These fields, of course, are in a province fully under China's control. But there are immense unexploited petroleum deposits over the line in Sinkiang—in the Wusu district—and toward these the great powers, Russia particularly, turn their eyes.

The one great contest for influence and control of Sinkiang, in fact, is the tug-of-war between Chungking and Moscow. And the best way to show how vital and chronic it is, and how it works, is to tell about two unusual warriors whom we shall call Ma and Sheng for short.

The story begins in the pregnant year 1932, when Ma—otherwise General Ma Chung-ying, a precocious Mohammedan youth from Kansu province—led a full-scale Moslem uprising in Sinkiang. While Franklin Roosevelt was whipping his New Deal into shape, while Hitler was grabbing power and grooming his Nazis for conquest and while Japan was polishing off Manchuria, the Boy General Ma stormed through Sinkiang in a succession of victories.

Also in 1932, Sheng—otherwise General Sheng Shih-tsai—was defeated by the Japanese in Manchuria and fled with his army into Soviet territory. Unmolested by the Russians, he retreated along the Trans-Siberian Railroad, looking for a place to call home, and fell upon Sinkiang. Without much difficulty he ousted the incumbent Chinese governor, who was highly unpopular—among other things, he had kidnaped the daughter of a leading Moslem, a mortal offense which helped expedite the Moslem uprising fomented by Ma. Sheng at once set about dealing with the revolt, but the Moslems continued to back the boy general. The fighting went on for more than a year, and in 1934 the conquering Ma was at the gates of Tihwa.

General Sheng now called on his Russian friends for protection, and a powerful column of the Red Army streamed over the border, joined issue with Ma, trounced him and sent him fleeing across the Province to Kashgar, near the Pamir Plateau.

Sheng was filled with gratitude and enthusiasm—until he found out the Reds had come with their baggage, to stay. He had become a mere puppet of the Moscow government. Because he had to he agreed to a sort of condominium with the Russians, who brought in administrators and "advisers" with alarming promptitude. By 1936 the Reds had taken over virtual control of all Sinkiang, which was still officially a province under the Chungking government. They built barracks for the Sinkiang police and army, which were directed by Russians in all but name, and spent large sums on factories, airfields and strategic roads.

Save for sporadic clashes with Moslems, the Reds remained unchallenged masters until the grim winter of 1941-42, when Stalin called on every available able-bodied man to resist the Nazis. With most of the Red troops withdrawn from Sinkiang to fight in the west, Governor Sheng saw a golden opportunity. During the siege of Stalingrad he arrested three of the four leading Soviet officials in the province and thirteen pro-Soviet district governors as well as great numbers of minor officials.

The Russians were expelled with their luggage, as they had come. But they had sunk their roots deep in those eight years; the Comrades were gone but their system was planted. Chungking sources claim that during the Soviet occupation close to 100,000 people were seized and nearly half of them were never heard of again. Among those jailed and tortured were missioners, both Catholic and Protestant. Other foreigners, and at least one Russian Orthodox priest, also were scooped up in the Russian net.

Some of the blame for the reign of terror fell on Sheng, a suspicious and treacherous man, and he now saw that he would still need outside support to remain in the saddle. So he proffered his allegiance to Chungking, which welcomed this development with generous financial assistance. Sheng used the money to import Chinese officials and teachers and to negotiate the purchase of Russian installations, factories and commercial concessions.

At bay before the Nazi attack, the Russians had to like it. But they were by no means through. They held a trump in the person of our friend Ma, who had been taken in by them as a friend after he fled in defeat to Kashgar. He was said to have been feted and brought to Moscow, where his former enemies became his interested instructors.

After victory at Stalingrad, Russia's bargaining power returned. Sinkiang's Moslems became restive again and Moscow asked Generalissimo Chiang to remove Sheng—otherwise, "trade and good relations between the two countries would suffer." In March, 1944, planes bombed Tihwa for ten days. A Chinese military officer told me that Japan's Rising Sun emblem was painted on their wings—but the design of the planes was Russian and no Japanese aircraft dared venture so far into the middle of Asia. While I was at Lanchow, two divisions of Chinese troops went through the Gateway to bolster Sheng and the Chungking regime. The Generalissimo soon found it expedient to remove Sheng. He brought him to Chungking and made him Minister of Forestry.

The governorship was given to Chu Shao-liang, who was apparently acceptable to Moscow but whose presence made little difference in the situation. Moslem nomads continued to murder Chinese, and someone continued to arm them with rifles and other military equipment in exchange for their sheep. In November, 1944, the city of Kuldja in the extreme west, on the Soviet border, was occupied by the rebels. This and other developments seemed to indicate that Ma, the boy general, was at it again—this time an older, more confident Ma.

3 . . . More About Sinkiang

STRANGE AS IT MAY SEEM, Sinkiang knew Christianity when most of Europe was still worshiping idols. And paradoxically, the first land of Cathay to know God through the Word of Christ has today a smaller number of Christians than any other province of China.

At some time in the early centuries, Nestorian Christians pushed their way over the great Silk Route to Sinkiang and into Western China. So many remains of churches and monasteries have been unearthed by explorers that it would seem half the population of Sinkiang had once been Christian.

When Marco Polo traveled the route from Venice to Peking, late in the thirteenth century, he found Nestorian Christians and a church at Kashgar in western Sinkiang. We learn from Polo that the son of Genghis Khan and uncle of Kublai Khan became a Christian and erected a great church in Kanchow, which he named after St. John the Baptist. Polo remained a year at Kanchow, at the eastern end of the Kansu Corridor, to learn all he could about the life, customs and history of the Tartars and their great Khan rulers. He found three churches and great numbers of Christians at Kanchow and tells of the bloody struggles they were then having with the Mohammedans. These eventually outnumbered and wiped out the Christians, whose churches disappeared like footprints in the Asiatic deserts.

Marco Polo went on to Peking, where he told the emperor about the wonders of Christian Europe, and the emperor sent word to the Pontiff in Rome asking for one hundred missioners. They were not sent at that time, but later the Franciscan John of Monte Corvino went to Peking and was followed by a small group of missioners. The Franciscans passed on, and for the next three hundred years no Christians went to China, which had closed her door to all foreigners. The Jesuits re-opened the door part way in the latter half of the sixteenth century, when they were welcomed at the Peking court. After that, missioners filtered in little by little and spread through the interior. The tide of favor turned for and against the Christians with different emperors. In the eighteenth century many Christians were banished from Peking to the colony of Chinese Turkestan, now Sinkiang. Franciscan missioners in Sian learned about them, and until 1879 one of them took the long trail through the Kansu Corridor every two years to visit them.

The distance from Sian to the farthest Christian outpost— Ili in western Sinkiang—was more than 2300 miles, or about the same as from New York to San Francisco. The Franciscans went by horsecart or rode mules or camels. Under the best conditions it took seventy-two days to get to Ili. Usually there were breakdowns and attacks by Moslems along the route. The priest plodded through deep snows and braved Central Asiatic blizzards through the winter months, baptizing the newborn and ministering to the Christians of Sinkiang. With the spring thaw, he started back on the three-month trip to Sian. Many of these priests never returned. Illness, accidents, storms and Moslems accounted for their loss.

In 1879 the Belgian Fathers took over from the Franciscans. They established headquarters in Lanchow and continued to send missioners over the long Kansu Corridor trail every two years. Ten years later two Belgian fathers were assigned to live in Sinkiang. They went out from Belgium through Russia, and there is an interesting note on their first contact with their Sinkiang flock. This was at Kuldja, just within the border. There were Russian Orthodox priests here who had repeatedly offered to minister to the Catholics in the intervals between visits of the Roman priests from Kansu. The faithful had declined what they considered a sacrilegious favor. Now, when they saw two priests coming from Russia instead of Kansu, they became suspicious. The elders held council and then put three tests to the newcomers: they were asked if they had wives, then to make the sign of the cross, then to recite the Hail Mary. They had no wives; they crossed themselves from left to right and they said the Hail Mary in Latin. Satisfied, the parishioners allowed them to enter Kuldja's little chapel and say Mass.

Belgian fathers lived and worked in Sinkiang for more than thirty years. Then, wishing to develop missions in Mongolia, they asked the Divine Word Fathers, who had more recruits, to take over the Kansu and Sinkiang work. And so in 1922 the last of the Christian missioners went up the Kansu Corridor in horsecarts from Lanchow.

They passed the places where Marco Polo had stayed—indeed, they journeyed no faster than he. The Nestorians and their churches had long since disappeared; instead, the new missioners found Christians who had been banished from Eastern China. As they inched their way west, week after week, they must have thought of those who had gone before and not returned; it is less likely that they had any foreboding of the persecution and torture in store for them a few years later. For seventy-four days they were stung by desert sands, scorched by the sun, jostled in the springless carts. They heard the drivers crack their whips and cuss heaven and earth and all between during the day, and at night they heard the wolves howl around the oasis.

There were eight of them, and they went to the cities and towns of the fertile Ili and Tihwa valleys, where most of Sinkiang's Chinese population had settled. This is in the upper half of the province; the lower half, beyond the Tienshan Mountains, is entirely Mohammedan. The missioners found the Chinese Christians a stanch lot. Most of them were descendants of Christians banished or persecuted because of their faith, and these clung to the church with the fanatical zeal of exiles who have battled for their convictions.

The earth was kind in the remote valleys. Its white blanket of snow invited rest and sleep in winter, but in summer it was prodigal with grains, grapes, apricots, apples, melons and all manner of vegetables. The missioners worked the land for exercise or pastime and kept a few cows for butter and milk. Deer and pheasant often capered to the gates of the missions —game was to be had for the asking. Moreover, the Moslem Kazaks and the nomad Mongols, who were herdsmen, were friendly. They kept the missions supplied with fermented mare's milk, a delicious summer beverage.

The Divine Word Fathers had considerable success in increasing their fold. As the number of converts grew to almost a thousand, more of their priests were sent to Sinkiang (most of them came from the Netherlands and Germany). In the early thirties eleven priests were in Sinkiang and many new chapels and stations had been built. Everything was serene, prosperous and more promising than ever in 1934, when the beleaguered Governor Sheng forged a thunderbolt with his SOS to the Russians.

After the Russians came and took control, a ghastly new chapter in Sinkiang's history began. Between 1934 and 1942 the prisons were jammed, suicide was common, terror clutched the people. Old-stock Christians went to jail and never came out; timid new converts kept silent about their belief, and some few denied it and turned traitors to the men who had sacrificed so much to befriend and instruct them. Thousands of Chinese were imprisoned; so were White Russians, Austrians, Germans, Italians, French and Rumanians.

Russian secret police were particularly active in their persecution of the Catholic and Protestant missioners, whom they
seemed to consider "foreign observers." They constantly
shadowed them; they arrested their servants and put spies in
their homes; they threatened Chinese Christians generally and
threw scores into jail, where they lingered for years without
trial. But systematic persecution and threats and restrictions
failed to drive out the missioners. So in July, 1939—at the time,
incidentally, when negotiations for the Moscow-Berlin friendship pact were going on—they rounded up the religious and
threw them into jail. Most of the priests were Germans, and
the OGPU agents, aided by Sheng's puppet police, tried to
make them confess they were spies for the Friedrichstrasse.
They failed to break them, and in 1941, after eighteen months
of jail and torture, the Divine Word Fathers, emaciated and
scarred in body and mind, were brought to the border of Kansu
in chains and shooed into the dubious freedom of exile. A very
short time after the clever OGPU had set these men free,
Hitler attacked Russia.

The missioners settled in Lanchow, awaiting the day when
they can return to Sinkiang. Not all the faithful were killed
or jailed, and not all those at liberty turned from the faith.
Courageous men and women remained in the great unhappy
land beyond the Kansu Corridor. From time to time a friendly
trader brought a message fifteen hundred miles to Lanchow,
telling the priests how their flock gathered secretly in this big
house or that to pray on feast days, or asking them to offer
a Mass for one who was ill or one who had died.

I spoke to these missioners and to others. Fifteen people
of five different nationalities told me of their experiences in
OGPU jails. A volume could be written from what they told
me in my few days at Lanchow. I will give only the story of
one Protestant and one Catholic missioner. These speak for all.

4 . . . A Protestant Hermit

THE PROTESTANT MISSIONER whose story I tell was George Hunter, a man my British friend Stanley Smith had strongly urged me to visit. I had no trouble finding him, for he lived on the grounds of the China Inland Mission. He dwelt in a one-room adobe shack, a veritable hermit's hovel, in an out-of-the-way corner of the compound. He was hanging woolen winter underwear to dry on a line outside his low door, when I approached.

A stooping, wiry little man with white bristles sticking up on his head and out from his jowls and chin, he regarded me with blue eyes whose candor was almost embarrassing. He was a type for the movies, dressed in an old red sweater over a lumberjack flannel shirt, with heavy, baggy trousers and sheepskin-lined slippers of soft leather, like those worn by nomad shepherds.

Mr. Hunter led me into his home—a room furnished with only a small bed, a table and two chairs, the sole luxury being a wallcase filled with an assortment of books relating to Central Asia. I spent the better part of two days visiting with him. But for the pressure of business, I would gladly have sat on the little hard chair, listening to this remarkable ancient, for weeks.

George Hunter was born in a small town near Aberdeen, Scotland, in 1862. He went out to the Orient in 1888—working with the China Inland Mission—and there he remained. The tough little Scot made many a strange choice during his career in China. He lived a celibate life—not from rule, for he is a

Protestant, but from choice. He felt a family and home would limit his labors, divide his singleness of purpose.

He went home for a visit in 1900, but that was the only time he left his work in the remote field of his choice. During his first dozen years he was in the Lanchow area, where he had the companionship of fellow missionaries and worked along in the ordinary way. But George Hunter was an extraordinary man; his spirit was restless treading the ordinary path. In these first few years he had learned of the great spaces to the west where no Protestant missionary had yet penetrated. He hungered for the pioneer work of felling trees, clearing the land and turning the soil for Christianity.

He knew, of course, that the people of Sinkiang were Mohammedans and Buddhists, Turks and Mongols, and various nomad tribes. It is an axiom that Mohammedans cannot be converted, and it is extremely difficult to convert a Buddhist. But Hunter refused to accept these generally recognized truths. One day he simply packed up and traveled two thousand miles west, to live and work alone in that vast, rough, mysterious land—Sinkiang.

Any place in China was thought to be isolated when Hunter first went out, half a century ago. There was a universal lack of postal and telegraph service and highroads. It took nearly three months to get by boat, by foot and by oxcart from Shanghai to Lanchow. But like the hermits of old who went to live in the desert, this man chose to lose himself to the world, shutting himself off in the farthest corner of China's hinterland. He set out on his journey in a two-wheeled horsecart to the far interior, three months distant from Lanchow.

Hunter had worked alone in Sinkiang for more than fifteen years when another missionary wrote to say he wished to join him. Hunter had not asked for an associate, fearing another man might be unable to bear the rigors of such a life, and he wrote back: "A man must be prepared to banish all thoughts of comfort and home if he would be a missionary in Sinkiang." The other accepted the conditions and came, but he "burned out in less than twenty years," and from then on Hunter remained alone.

He claimed affiliation with no special denomination, saying, "I am interested only in humanity, in bringing the message of Christianity to the most forgotten people." If we figured the success of his labor in numbers or other tangible evidence, the result might appear disappointing. But if we view his labor as courage, sacrifice and perseverance, it is the success of the saints: he went to plow and sow the seed, and with that he felt his work was done. In his mind the simple message of Christianity was so appealing that he considered it was enough just to pass it on to others.

During the long winters, when the snows were deep, he spent his time writing grammars and dictionaries of the tribal languages of Middle Asia. With the melting of the snows, he was off on the road to spread his gospel until the first fall blizzards drove him back to Tihwa. Sitting astride a hardy little horse, he traveled all over the province and beyond its borders. One summer before the First World War he went over the Ural Mountains, within a few hours' train ride of Moscow. Working with the nomad tribes that followed herds of sheep and cattle, he lived in their round, cowhide tents or pitched his own beside them and told them about Christianity.

George Hunter stuck by his task through rebellions, civil wars, earthquakes and the first calamitous years of Soviet control in Sinkiang. The summer that the Reds started rounding up missioners, he was off in the hills somewhere with the tribes and wasn't molested. But the winter of 1941 came and he returned to his place in Tihwa. Late one evening a group of Russian secret police broke in on him with drawn revolvers, searched his house from top to bottom—while they kept him covered like a criminal—and then whisked him off to prison.

He was then seventy-eight years old. When he asked the Russian officer for an explanation, he was told, "You are a spy, and it is our duty to shoot spies."

The story of his torture and imprisonment for eighteen months is long and horrifying.

"My friends would not believe some of the fantastic things I went through," he said.

I told him I had already heard similar stories from a dozen other victims of Communist zeal, and he settled down to relate how he had swung between life and death, between sanity and insanity, for a year and a half.

"Once I was inside the prison," he said, "they put into action their methods of deranging my mind to the point of making me admit I was a British spy and sign a confession."

First they starved him for two days; then they started the no-sleep torture. He was forced to stand for days without sleep until his mind wandered into semi-consciousness and delirium. Then they would ask him to write a confession saying he was a spy employed by the British government. He remained stubbornly silent, and his tormentors would repeat every now and then, "Good night, Mr. Hunter; hope you sleep well."

After days without sleep, and with a starvation diet of Russian cabbage soup and hard black bread, Hunter felt insanity approaching. "It was a kind of mental intoxication and delirium," he told me. "The psychology of their method is to weaken the mental faculties so much that truth cannot be withheld." Police in foreign lands have found fault with the method, in that, if a man's mental powers are weakened too much, he becomes irrational and will admit false accusations as the truth. If carried far enough, the torture forces a complete surrender of will—a man can be made to say whatever his torturers want him to say.

Threats were added to the no-sleep treatment. Guns were

placed on the table when the Russian judge questioned Hunter. During the questioning, shots would be fired in other parts of the prison and guards would name off to him the servants or converts or friends who were being executed by those shots. They would take his mail as it came in, tear it up in front of him, and say the letters referred to spy work. They tore up the money they found on him and in his house in retaliation for some alleged crime. One day when shots were fired outside they told him, "There go your two horses"—his only constant companions.

He remembered signing several papers. He doesn't know what they were, only that it was what they wanted him to say. "I don't know," he told me. "Probably one of the things they forced me to sign was a confession of espionage."

After that, he was put back in his cell and given food and sleep. They put a loudspeaker out of sight near his cell, and from a record ran off the questions and answers of his trial. As he heard his own voice making unbelievable statements, agonizing doubts of his sanity returned. They had forced some of his converts and servants to testify against him, and the record of this they also put through the speaker to stab his heart and upset his mind.

Part of the time he was kept in a prison so crowded that the inmates had to take turns lying down to rest. His companions were a motley collection—Koreans, Turki Moslems, Chinese, even a Russian Orthodox priest. "We had been stripped of all our possessions," he said, "and the Mohammedans missed their beads. Whenever they got bread that was soft enough they pinched out pieces of dough and rolled them into pellets, stringing them on what little bits of string they could find, then set them aside to dry. When they were hard, they fingered them with great reverence and satisfaction." (Imprisoned Catholics, I learned, made rosaries in this manner.)

The guards often came in to taunt Hunter and the Russian priest, mocking at Christianity and sneering, "All the other missionaries have been shot—your turn will come next." The old man said that what hurt him most was the "constant mockery of God—the shameless blasphemies spoken against Him." These men were "more like demons than humans. I thought then and I think now that this whole Soviet activity is directed by the Evil One himself."

In the final months of his bondage, he said, he had little or no control over his mind: "I kept hearing voices—the voices of my tormentors and the voices of former friends testifying against me."

A woman doctor who examined him from time to time told her superiors in the summer of 1942 that the eighty-year-old prisoner was in danger of dying, and he was removed to a hospital. His strength was built up for two months, then he was summarily banished from the land in which he had toiled without rest or thought of self for half a century. Still tottering with weakness, he was put on a truck which bumped along the desert trail for two weeks and finally deposited him in Lanchow.

For months after his release, he said, he still heard the voices of his torturers and the loudspeakers taunting him with his own insane lies. Many things that he told me he asked me not to repeat—and in deference to his wishes I have left them out. He frequently asked me if I believed his statement, if I thought he was in his right mind. I had no doubt—you could have no doubt, looking into George Hunter's clear, candid eyes —and I told him so.

I was sorry when I had to leave this man, who at eighty-three sat increasing his book knowledge of Central Asia and writing religious tracts for the people, while he dreamed of the day when his exile would end and he would be able to resume his labors in the hinterland. He even asked me to pull strings in Chungking so he could obtain a visa to get back to Sinkiang right away. For a man of his age the word "impossible" flashed through my mind, but I caught it on the tip of my tongue—for it is men like Hunter who do the impossible.

5 . . . The Diary of Father Moritz

GEORGE HUNTER WAS one of many I interviewed in Lanchow who had survived the torture. The climactic chapter in this grim story, which haunted me as I tossed through a sleepless night, was the diary of Father Philip Moritz. He, Msgr. Loy, Father Hilbrenner, George Hunter and others had told me their startling experiences as we talked. Now Father Moritz remarked that during his captivity he had made notes which he destroyed, but he had rewritten the whole thing immediately after his release. He got out the diary at my request. I could not pause until I had read through to the end. Then I reread it and asked if I could make a copy. It is given here in an exact translation from the German.

It was Friday, July 14, 1939, just a little before nine in the evening, when the dogs began barking fiercely. I stepped out of the kitchen and caught sight of a man coming over the roof of one of our houses bordering the neighbor's property. I challenged him but received no answer. Quickly he managed to get down from the roof and boldly walked right up to me. He was a member of the police force.

I asked him what he wanted, but without a word of explanation he seized me by the arm and drew me along with him toward the entrance gate of the mission compound. Again asking him the reasons for such conduct, I found him so tense and excited that he was unable to answer. When he opened the large entrance door of the compound, I suddenly stood

face to face with a sizable force of policemen, with drawn
revolvers; some were in plain clothes, some in uniform. As a
disarming gesture, I nonchalantly told them I had been awaiting them.

The police entered, taking me along with them to my
residence. They posted guards all over the place. Shortly the
Chief of Police arrived.

"We have orders from the Provincial Government to search
the residence."

"The place is at your disposal," I replied.

It was just nine in the evening when the search began,
and almost noon next day when it ended. The police did a
thorough job, to judge from the looks of things after they had
finished. Every book, magazine or piece of paper that bore
some writing was collected, packed together and promptly
taken to the police headquarters for examination. The search
over, they advised me to get together a few personal things
as I would have to leave my mission station of Suiting and
accompany them to the capital of the province of Kuldja,
thirty miles away.

Since it was the middle of July, I asked, "What kind of
clothing and how much shall I take along?"

"Just your summer clothes," they replied.

Foolishly enough I followed their advice and left behind
all winter clothes and thick bedding, though they would have
been most useful in the coming days of distress. Too late I
came to realize the real intention of the authorities in my
regard.

They sealed all doors and boxes in Chinese style (by past-
ing long strips of paper with writing on them across the open-
ings). As soon as it was dark an auto drew up at the entrance
of the mission. The police seemed to have waited for darkness
in order to cover up their actions and not to arouse suspicion.
From the waiting car, the Chief of Police, an aide and a Rus-

sian stepped forth, walked into the mission compound, made
some plans for the protection of the station, placed guards at
several points, then took me with them into the car for the
drive to Kuldja and to prison.

I was thrown into a six by eight cell. The furniture consisted of an iron bed with some boards on it. They called my
attention to their great consideration in having the bed placed
there especially for me. A small window facing the courtyard
admitted a little light but offered no view to the exterior. A
chair was later added to the furnishings of my new home.
It likewise served as a table at mealtime.

The food given me during the first days was the same as
that of the other prisoners: mornings for breakfast, tea and dry
bread; at noon came nasty-tasting Russian vegetable soup and
bread. That was all. Several days of this was more than enough,
so I asked the warden for Chinese food, with the result that
an extra dish of vegetables was added to the old fare. Later
on a little sugar was served for the tea. With a little money
left to me, I was permitted to buy some fruit.

During the day the guards allowed me the freedom of the
courtyard for about twenty minutes. Things were gradually
improving, I thought; and when they actually allowed me to
use the Russian bath located in the officers' quarters, I became
convinced of it.

To my surprise a Russian woman doctor visited me one
day and asked whether I had any physical complaints. I informed her that from birth I had suffered from poor nerves.
She put me through an investigation and wrote out a prescription according to her findings.

The monotony of prison life tries one's spirit and puts the
nerves on edge. The mind somehow becomes keenly active,
the senses alert. One day I heard a distant voice and recognized it at once as that of Father Oirschot. I realized then

that I was not the only S.V.D. in prison. Evidently the authorities staged the same "play" in other mission stations as in mine.

The night of August 23, after six weeks of imprisonment, I was roused from deep sleep by the noisy clanking of my prison door. An officer stepped in and asked me in a rather friendly tone to rise and accompany him. By this time the prisoners were quite familiar with the clinking sound of unlocking, opening doors, and knew what it meant.

I went with the officer to the court of the Assistant Chief of Police, who happened to be a Russian, Uglin by name.

He began by asking me, "Have you ever held any political office?"

"No, I have not."

"But you have been an army officer."

"Yes, that was during the First World War; then we all were soldiers."

Carefully the questions and answers were noted down to be delivered to the office of the Protocol.

Producing a Chinese letter written on red paper, Uglin inquired, "Do you know anything about this?"

"No, I do not. Please have it read to me."

Upon Uglin's direction, the interpreter read the letter. It had been addressed to the Catholic Mission and dealt with the sale of hides and wool.

"I am not acquainted with the letter," I asserted.

"This letter has been found in your room." Uglin grinned.

Suddenly I recalled the existence of a letter written on red paper that lay stuck in one of my books, where it served as a bookmark. The letter happened to be there when the book was brought to Suiting some time ago. I explained further that I had never taken the trouble of reading the letter, but I knew that Father Hufnagel, deceased several years previously, had carried on correspondence with a concern on the coast at Tientsin as far back as 1923. This German company, handling such merchandise as hides and wool, was interested in the Sining market and wanted to find out the prevailing prices and the business possibilities. Evidently this red-paper letter was an answer to their inquiries.

"That's what you say," Uglin commented sarcastically, "but we know nothing about that."

"I am speaking simply and honestly. That ought to be sufficient."

"This letter was found in the drawer of your writing desk," he said with firmness and conviction. He was looking me coldly in the eye. "It shows plainly that *you are a spy*."

"If I were a spy, and the letter a potential proof of espionage, do you think I would be so foolish as to let it remain in the writing desk?"

"You had no other way out," he laughed.

I laughed just as loud, but he didn't like it a bit.

To cover up, he rose, came toward me and began an appealing discourse. Most of it I failed to understand, though I did grasp the gist of it: the letter pointed out clearly that I was a spy.

The Russian, Uglin, then drew forth another letter, written by a certain Mr. Beick shortly before he committed suicide. How it happened that I kept that silly letter, which should have been destroyed immediately upon receipt, is more than I can explain. Still, there wasn't anything to be feared from the contents except for one unfortunate sentence which Beick wrote in his insanity. It read: "The Catholic Church is a secret organization and is responsible for my death."

"There you have it," said Uglin. "That clearly shows that you are all spies."

"Hold on, Mr. Uglin," I pleaded. "That's what you say. But have you ever heard what type of man Mr. Beick was and what the Catholic Church did for him? Mr. Beick, afflicted with syphilis of the third stage, partially lost the use of his mental faculties. The Church took him in and ministered to him. Dr. Buss at our mission station remarked that such victims suffer from softening of the brain and often end up as suicides. So it happened with Mr. Beick, who shot himself after a steadily growing mental upheaval."

Uglin dropped the Beick case and made no further mention of it. Yet it seemed very plain that the Russian aimed to stop at nothing in branding me as a spy. Once more he dug down into his files and produced a document that seemed to inflate his confidence.

"Here is another charge against you," he leered. "I should like to hear you answer it. A certain Father Kolomb, stationed at Suiting, held meetings of spies. Later when you took over his place you assumed leadership of this espionage unit. Now confess and tell us the whole truth about your activities."

"These are the facts: Father Kolomb told me on my arrival at Suiting that he had organized a co-operative for the benefit of the poor working class. Conditions, however, were anything but favorable. Great obstacles continued to arise. He left it to my judgment to carry on or to break up the unit. I chose the latter, the group disintegrated, and that was the end of it."

Uglin's files continued to produce fantastic accusations, but now of a more personal, intimate stamp.

"There can be no further doubt of your being a spy," Uglin began. "We have here the evidence of no other than Mr. Wang-che-yi, the personal servant of Father Kolomb, and also the testimonies of Messrs. Kolozof and Belorussoff [two White Russians] and others. These people have stated under oath that they were in your employ and that you are a spy."

"Anyone can make false accusations, but it's another thing to prove them!"

Though seeming unperturbed, Uglin realized his charges had thus far fallen flat. He felt himself forced to redeem the situation. He began to pull out the "trump cards" that he had reserved till he was compelled to play them.

"Your espionage game is up and you might just as well confess now, or we will be forced to put you on the spot."

"I have nothing to confess." Though I had no idea what charges would be made next, I was prepared to bear down on everything.

"Very well, then. Here is the name of a certain Mr. Max Unger. Do you know him?"

"Most certainly."

"And would you care to hear what he has to say about you?"

"Gladly, sir."

Presently Mr. Unger stepped into the room. Very well known to our missionaries, he had been a high official of the largest leather company in Kuldja for the last twenty-five years. He had been sent to prison three months before the same fate befell me.

Uglin asked whether we still knew each other and whether we were still on good terms. Both of us gave friendly assent. Then Uglin urged him to give his testimony in my regard. To my great amazement, Mr. Unger stated that he had performed acts of espionage for both Father Kolomb and me.

"Give an example," prompted Uglin, to this embarrassed fabricator.

Mr. Unger then related that I had visited him at Kuldja in 1937 just when the captured revolutionaries were being brought in. He declared that I inquired the names of those who had been captured. Moreover, when planes arrived from Russia at the same time in order to protect Kuldja, I immediately showed interest in the planes and their numbers as well as in the airfield and its size. When I asked to look over the field, he told me it would not be possible because of the heavy guard.

All this got under my skin. I turned toward him abruptly and asked him to his face what sort of lying testimony this was meant to be.

Unger turned away, and the Russian Uglin burst forth with a thundering roar: "I do the questioning here. No one else!"

Unger was led away out of sight.

It is true that I had paid Unger a visit at Kuldja, but our conversation touched simply on general conditions and current events. No mention was made of prisoners and airfields. More and more I pitied him and forgave him from the bottom of my heart.

Uglin, unyielding, continued aiming his guns at me. His ammunition seemed never to give out. Once more he began:

"Do you know a certain Chalize?"

"Chalize? The name is unfamiliar. Does the person go by any other name?"

"Yes," Uglin replied. "The gentleman is also known as Chen-yu-jen."

"Oh, yes! That name is known to me."

"Well, then, shall I also have him called in to give his personal testimony? He, too, has confessed aiding your espionage game. You must remember."

"Call him in. I may as well hear them all."

Chen-yu-jen, a Mohammedan, possessed a really fine character. He was in the medicine business and often came to me for a visit or for advice. I had warned him that the police were watching my visitors and he had better be careful. He was finally apprehended and thrown into prison three weeks before me.

Chen stepped in and testified he had been a spy in my employ, receiving as much as one hundred dollars a month. When asked to give an example, he coined the lie that I had sent him to the motor freight terminal to investigate the amount of hides and wool transported from Sinkiang to Russia.

Challenging this padded evidence, I flatly denied every false statement. With a vehemence hard to control, I declared that the lying Chen was never in my employ in any way, never received a cent from me.

Uglin called to my attention that the statements of personal witnesses could not possibly be false, since, by their open confessions, they indicted themselves.

Being at bay, I could not answer back what I realized only too well to be true: that these unfortunate accusers were forced under threat of torture and even death to tell deliberate untruths. This became crystal clear to me later on, when I, too, had to go through the grilling torture in the execution of which the Russian Communists are past masters.

Turning to Uglin, I stated bluntly that if he handled my case strictly in accord with justice I should have nothing to fear. But if, on the other hand, he was resolved to give credence to the lying statements of my accusers I should have to suffer innocently.

Unimpressed, Uglin wound up with a little speech in a quite sympathetic tone, appealing to my sense of honor to confess and declare the truth.

By the time I was led away from the courtroom a new day was dawning. This time I was not taken to my prison cell but to a room in the courthouse. The jailers told me to be seated on a chair in the corner. After allowing me a short rest they began taunting me, saying over and over again, "You might as well confess. There is no sense in trying to hold out."

The hours of the day passed. Still I sat, gritting my teeth and trying to hold out. No bit of food was allowed to reach me. Growing weak and weary I desired to rest. The night came on and passed and still no food, no rest. I was permitted to sit, walk or stand but not to sleep or recline. The jailers changed shifts and the new force took up with fresh vigor.

In the morning the Chief of Police, a Chinese, arrived. I complained that I had not been allowed to sleep or eat for the last forty hours.

"Oh," he remarked, "three or four days without sleep means nothing, but food you shall have."

Food was soon served. From then on the meals came with regularity. I realized now what I was up against. I was going through the Russian "no-sleep torture."

Day and night the jailers carried on their verbal assaults: "You might as well confess. Holding out will do no good." Often they would add, "So far everyone has confessed, and you cannot sleep until you have done so."

All the guards were charged with the duty of vexing and harassing their prisoner. Almost without letup they kept right on hurling questions at me and impatiently demanding a response. Every word spoken was taken down and sent to the office of the Protocol.

After several days and nights of this incessant questioning, the torture began to produce its inevitable effects. I started to fancy things, living in a dream. Dazed and unconscious I would walk into tables and chairs or out of the room. When I was aroused by the call of my name or by ramming into an obstruction, presence of mind would snap back once more. As time went on the mental confusion grew steadily worse.

After holding out for several days, the thought came to me I should yield to their demands. But when the Chief of Police came in to force a confession my resistance unconsciously stiffened.

"Who among your Christians was the weakest in the faith?" the Chief bluntly asked.

"How can you expect me to testify against my people in such matters?" I answered.

"Tell me," he continued. "To whom have you spoken about the political affairs of this province?"

In the mental fog that beset me, I thought I could give names without harm to anyone. Fagged and perplexed, I blurted out the names of several Christian families of Suiting.

"And what districts of the province have you visited?" the Chief asked.

I named a town near the Russian border. Immediately he showed interest.

"What was your business there?" he demanded.

"Oh," I replied, "that was the home of my tailor." How little I realized then that I would be responsible for an obscure tailor's prompt arrest and imprisonment!

Uglin, the chief's assistant, next appeared on the scene, producing a note written in Russian. Though I did not understand it I believed it to be a transcript of the preceding conversation and consented to add my signature. Such is the fiendishness of the no-sleep torture, that it unbalances the mental forces and twists the will so that the victim readily signs whatever is presented.

After I had signed, Uglin evidently thought he had reached the point where he could make me talk as he would. This time he came forward with a large sheet of paper and asked me to name all the spies that I employed in the places listed on the paper.

Then the mental shadows suddenly lifted. With full consciousness restored, momentarily at least, I gave way to indignation. Looking him squarely in the eyes I sputtered with emphasis, "What do you mean? I never had any spies. Let this end now, once and for all!"

Uglin flared up. The Chief of Police, who stood near by taking in the scene, came up to join the verbal battle. Both let loose a flood of words that would have drowned out a loudspeaker. They ended up by stating that in their kindness they would still allow me some time to think it over.

Roughly I was ushered out of the court to the torture room

again. Suddenly the tears broke forth and I cried like a baby
for some time. Regaining self-control and realizing my conduct, I felt blushingly ashamed of myself. I apologized to the
group standing around and deplored that I could not help it.
Strangely, their iciness seemed to melt. With a shadow of
sympathy they offered me some water and a towel. But my
sleepless trial still continued.

My nerves were being taxed so severely that I found myself becoming jittery. Almost unconsciously I would reply to
all questions hurled at me, "I have nothing to confess. I am
innocent."

My stubborn holding out at times roused the impatience
and fury of my torturers. The Chief of Police stepped up front
and bellowed in my face, "You refuse to speak? Well, we have
other methods that will loosen your tongue."

"Torture me as you like," I responded, "even unto death.
Then you will have gained your end."

"We have means, even without inflicting death," he said
angrily.

Later in the day one of the chief's officials asked me for
the names of those who belonged to the co-operative unit
organized by my predecessor, Father Kolomb.

Perhaps a little better than half conscious, I consented to
name several members. Under a strange impulse, unchecked
by my numbed intellect, I leaned over and whispered, "I
know something better. At my residence in Suiting there is
a book with all the names you want. Then you will know
everything. But don't tell Uglin. Take me to Suiting and we
can get the list."

"Exactly where is the book hidden?" he asked with awakened interest.

When I told him the place, he regarded me for a while
and then warned, "This trip must produce results without fail,
or else due punishment will follow."

It was a relief to get out of the jail for the thirty-mile ride from Kuldja to Suiting, even in the pitch-black of night. I led the way to the book's hiding place. But the precious, promised book could nowhere be found. I felt embarrassed and more confused than ever. The two rascals, however, thought they had been fooled and took out their spite on me all the way back to Kuldja.

The following morning, when the Chief of Police learned of our escapade, he did not flare up but invited me to accompany him to Suiting in a few days for another investigation of the mission compound. He seemed to sense that I meant no trickery and believed the book might still be found.

Readily I agreed, anxious to get away from jail at any opportunity and to forget my sleeplessness.

Before dismissing me from his office, the Chief of Police questioned pointedly, "Father Kolomb had an archive. Can you tell me where it is?"

"To show that we have no secrets I can tell you exactly where to find it." I had hidden it to protect my parishioners.

My description of the archive location seemed to gratify the chief. He returned me to my torture quarters.

Two days later I was bumping along on the highroad to Suiting again. This time, Uglin, the assistant chief, joined the party. The archive was found exactly as I had described and was thoroughly investigated. Even more of the flooring than necessary was torn up to make sure that no shred of evidence might be overlooked.

Once more the rooms of the mission station were turned topsy-turvy. Any book or magazine that had been overlooked at the first search was now taken along; also my photo album.

Days gave way to nights, and nights to days, and yet my sleepless torture went on. The spells of delirium became more frequent and lasted longer. At last I came to the stage where I hardly recognized my own room.

About the tenth day of my no-sleep torture a new guard was added to the staff. Named Hu Chih Tung, his past was more than a little colorful. He had originally been sent to Sinkiang as a spy for the Central Government of China. Discovered by the Communists, he was sent to Tihwa and after four months of prison was brought to trial. Tortured in various ways, he finally broke down and consented to join hands with the Sinkiang Government, working as a spy for the Communists.

Hu Chih, though perhaps good at heart, could be mean and nasty. He set upon me with all his wily energy to break me down. He would force me to sit, to stand and to pace up and down in rapid succession, repeating the same process hour after hour till I simply couldn't move my limbs any longer. My nerves were just about finished, my mental powers exhausted and my physical energy at the point of collapse, so that I stumbled drunkenly at every step.

Like a keyhole of light in a dark room, a sudden thought penetrated my blacked-out brain: "Why go on? You are accomplishing nothing! You cannot change their conviction that you are a spy! Give in to their demands and you will have rest. *Rest!*"

The idea pounded and pounded for attention. It seemed to be the only thing to do, for all balanced judgment had fled.

The next morning, when interpreter Wang appeared, I asked for pen and paper. Laboriously I tried to write.

"When I left Paderborn for China I received a commission from a certain 'Ventus' to send him detailed information about Kansu. Later on, at Sining, I carried on some espionage, but never in Sinkiang."

Wang received the statement, flustered with excitement, and dashed off to the chief's office. In a moment he returned with Uglin.

"What were the names of those you dealt with at Sining?" Uglin demanded.

"Will this questioning never end? Will I never get any rest?" Disgusted and exasperated I gave whatever names came to mind.

Uglin felt he had me where he wanted me and kept on plying me with questions all morning and all afternoon to extract every possible bit of information. Finally Uglin and Wang accompanied me to my prison cell and gave the warden special orders to treat me well.

Thus, after eleven days of torture, sleep came at last. What a relief and luxury it was, even on the hard boards of the iron bed! Needless to say I was sound asleep within a few seconds. After two hours I was awakened and led back and forth in the open yard, lest too deep a sleep prove harmful, like food after a hunger strike.

After that first night of blessed sleep, I felt mentally though not yet physically refreshed. But with the return of my five senses, I also began to realize what I had done and bitter regret set in. What could I do, I wondered, to repair the harm I might have done to the mission. As the gravity of my offense seemed to grow more serious the more I thought of it, my former physical tortures appeared as nothing in comparison. Foolishly, though unwittingly, I had stepped from one kind of torture into another.

Toward evening, after a day of self-accusation, I was told that a warm bath had been prepared for me in another cell. Soon I heard a familiar voice, the voice of Father Oirschot. The bath became a matter of secondary importance and of slow progress as we whispered our stories through a fissure in the wall separating us. Briefly but rapidly I related my experiences and my present confusion, consulting his advice.

The following day found me once again at peace, for I had resolved to retract at the first opportunity all I had said and written, no matter what the cost might be. The missionary may be allowed to suffer, but never the mission cause.

For forty-eight hours I rested, building up courage and energy but not yet revealing my intention of retracting. It was the night of September 3, at the end of the second day's rest, that I was summoned to the courtroom. How different now the atmosphere of the court! There was an air of friendliness reflected on every face. Uglin and interpreter Wang began the usual interrogations about my spy activities. Their smooth conduct seemed so out of character that I could scarcely believe my eyes and ears.

Without yielding in the least to their high-powered charm, I frankly and curtly declared that I had nothing to report. Questions and answers followed in endless flow. Mild, gentle pleadings were followed by obstinate denials, but in a calm conversational tone throughout.

The hour of eleven at night had struck when I was led away from court, but not to my own cell. Back in the old torture chamber once more, the second act of my passion was about to begin. Evidently Uglin was not satisfied with the results achieved. Continued "treatment," he thought, would produce the desired effect.

Wasting no time I called for pen and paper. With the greatest willingness the articles were proffered. Evidently it was surmised that, face to face with the prospect of new tortures, I must have weakened. My real intention was hardly suspected.

In retraction of my former "confession," I wrote: "Let it be known that I hereby retract all my previous written statements regarding spy activities. I wrote a wholly false confession only under severe torture that distorted my judgment and robbed me of all sense of responsibility. Furthermore, I hereby declare that never at any time in my life have I received a commission from any country to carry on any sort of espionage."

As I relaxed, Wang stepped over and asked what I had written. When I explained, he grew red with anger and declared that I was trying to make them appear fools. He rushed the statement to Uglin and the second act began in earnest.

To begin with, I was forced to walk or to stand continually, with only brief periods of sitting. For twenty-four long hours of each day the sleepless treatment continued. For the first four days I received neither food nor drink of any kind. Beginning on the fifth day a little bread and some tea was allowed for my daily subsistence. Only on rare days was a little extra bread and a little soup added to the frugal diet.

Even the brief spells of sitting were gradually diminished, then canceled entirely. The muscles of my feet and legs began to redden and swell. The pain was almost unbearable. This method brought results much faster than the first act. Then I usually became delirious only at night, except toward the end of the eleven-day period, when I scarcely ever snapped out of it. But now, in the second act, delirium came on much earlier in the day. I began talking all kinds of nonsense with the guards. Weird images rushed through my brain. I fancied a young man was seated in my room at a typewriter. At first I thought he must be in my service and then came to suspect he must be a spy sent to watch me. Something drove me to seek escape. I lunged for an exit but crashed into the bulk of a young Russian. I roared that I had to go out, he should get out of the way. Forcing my way I must have poked or slapped him in the face, for later he testified that I had struck him.

The Russian retaliated with several powerful punches in the chest. Inflated with his prowess he began more than ever to lord it over the despised priest.

Later, when I complained of the attack to the Chief of

Police: "That's what you get for not listening to orders," he replied.

From this point my real torture began. Uglin took great delight in beating me on the head and over the ears with a stick. Regularly I took his pommeling like a punching bag. My ears would swell and my head felt like an aching ball, covered with bumps.

Having made the mistake of signing one false confession, I was determined in sane moments never again to write a single false word—even if it cost me my life. But resolutions meant little to me now, with body, nerves and mind shattered. Once more the fixed idea took hold of me that I must make some sort of statement.

I confided to my guard Hu Chih that I had never been a spy and could therefore make no true confession of espionage. Would it be all right, I asked, if I wrote merely from imagination?

Hu Chih readily consented. Wang, the interpreter, at first disagreed, insisting that I write nothing but the truth. After the two had put their heads together, however, I was told to sit down and write at will.

Relishing the luxury of a seat, I wrote at a leisurely pace. This time my statement differed totally from my first "confession," written after the first eleven days of torture. When at length I had finished I was led by Hu Chih and Wang to Uglin's office. Handing the paper to Uglin I mentioned that Hu Chih had agreed to my writing this statement.

Uglin asked at once what that meant.

Hu Chih admitted that he had allowed my indulgence in fancies. He and Wang signed the paper and placed it before Uglin for his signature. Springing up in rage, Uglin tore the "confession" to shreds and began scolding and beating me. Hu Chih and Wang in a quick turn-about assumed the same attitude. They rushed me back to the torture chamber, beat and kicked me till they grew tired.

Malice and scorn marked their conduct toward me thereafter. Hu Chih, in particular, tortured me at every turn. When he chanced to be eating melons with his comrades he would thrust the rinds into my face or wash my face with the squashy inner rind.

On one occasion he took half of a melon unfit to eat, crowned my head with a smash, and roared with laughter as the juicy pulp ran down my face and clothing. Other times he would take his hot tea and sprinkle it all over me till the pot was emptied. But one of his most heartless devices was aimed at my beard. He would pull at it, twist it or tie strings to it, and then—without the least feeling or sympathy—jerk at the strings to pull out clusters of hair. My tears and my cries for mercy meant nothing. Even Wang, the interpreter, enjoyed the torment, though he contented himself with merely being an onlooker. Uglin regarded the whole procedure with no apparent interest or concern.

Next, they compelled me to hold my hands high up in the air until my arms fell absolutely limp to my sides. At another time they forced me to stretch my arms straight out from the shoulders until the blood seemed to leave my face. With my nerves already on edge for sheer want of sleep, and with my whole constitution undermined by the continuous strain, I sank to the floor in an almost complete blackout.

All logical thought and control of words seemed to escape me. I began saying things that could have cost me dear. What surprises me particularly is that the officials made no attempt to stop me.

One weary day passed after another. I was becoming alarmingly weak. Although I can recall only two falls to the floor, I know that my knees and elbows were seriously bruised.

The authorities were plainly perplexed as I refused to give

in. Their tricks and threats were met with the one answer, "I have nothing to confess." They beat me black and blue. They man-handled me in many disgraceful ways, as though I were less than a human being.

Uglin and the Chief of Police approached me one day and said (first in Russian and then in Chinese), "You have held out so long and allowed your health to suffer. However, there is still a chance for you. But if you choose to continue in your stubborn refusals your health will suffer so seriously that it cannot be restored. Be wise and confess now."

"I know what you say is true, but I have nothing to confess. I have never been a spy."

Day and night I continued to stand on my feet and suffer. My endurance seemed to be stretched to the limit. The officials stepped in once more to look me over. Apparently they reached the decision that it would be better to have no confession than to end up with a corpse on their hands.

Reluctantly they sent me back from the torture chamber to my prison cell, where I was permitted a few days of rest. These passed all too quickly, but I began to feel almost normal again.

The second phase of my passion—if I may call it that—was over. I wondered when the next act would take place. I did not have long to wait, for on the morning of the fifth day interpreter Wang appeared at the door and ordered me to leave the prison cell. "The first time," he said, "you were on your feet for eleven days, and the second time for sixteen days. Would you care to make it twenty-six days this time?"

I had entered the third and last phase of what seemed like hell on earth. During the first four days, neither food nor drink reached me. After that, the meals and the general procedure were very much the same as during the two previous ordeals. This time, however, the guards, apparently tired of the whole business, tortured me less than before. From the continual standing day and night, the swelling of my feet and legs set in very soon. My mind, too, slipped into a whirlpool of confusion much sooner than during the first two periods of torture.

I must have been standing for over a week without rest or sleep when the strange fixed idea again took hold of me that I should make some sort of false confession. With what little mental power remained to me I managed to concoct a story which, when dictated in Chinese, read substantially as follows: "In 1934, when I happened to be in Suchow, the Consul General called me to the German Consulate and asked me to send him detailed news about the state of affairs in the Sinkiang Province. But when I arrived at my destination and learned of the conditions prevailing there I wrote back to state that I could not comply with the wishes of the Consulate."

The Chief of Police stepped in to read the "confession." He looked at me suspiciously and asked whether the statement was true. At first I gave an evasive answer. The Chief gave me no rest, however, until I finally admitted that the statement was false. He made a sour face, puckered up his lips and with an air of disgust told me to write down my statement in my own hand.

Wang, the interpreter, stood by but had no idea what I was writing. When the script was finished, he immediately brought it to Uglin, who read it and translated it into his own language down to the last sentence, which stated that the self-accusation was positively false. Hu Chih, upon hearing the closing remark, set upon me with violent fury, striking my aching limbs everywhere with powerful fists and kicking me in places one would not even think of kicking a dog.

Wang, the interpreter, took over once more and ordered me to rewrite my statement, leaving out the last sentence. To gain time and rest, I wrote very slowly, repeating over and over again the same nonsensical sentence, "It is not true, is true." No doubt more blows and punishment would be in store for me, but I had reached the stage where pain had become second nature, so to say. I seemed to feel indifferent to whatever lay ahead of me, even death itself.

After about an hour of scribbling, I turned in the statement, calling it a job done perhaps for better but more likely for worse.

The Chief of Police, after studying the silly script, evidently advised his assistant Uglin that no further pressure be forced upon me and that I be sent back to prison, for soon I was on my way out of the torture chamber. I was a sick man, but, oh, how good it felt to be back in prison and allowed to remain at peace! How I thanked my God for the sleep and rest that now came to me! If this comfort was so sweet, I thought, what must heaven be like?

The number of days in the third and last phase of the no-sleep torture is not clear to me, but I am certain that the entire ordeal covered no less than thirty-seven days and nights of continual standing.

A few boards on the damp floor of my dark, stuffy, six by six cell were my bed and my only furniture. A few days later, thanks to a most unexpected display of mercy, my bed planks were raised off the floor and placed on two wooden horses. The daily fare handed out to the prisoners consisted of some bread and tea in the morning, some watery soup and bread at noon and in the evening. The plague of fleas, bedbugs and lice was simply terrible.

The October nights grew noticeably colder. I begged for some clothing, but nothing was forthcoming. To the two thin blankets an old torn quilt was added, but even this did not help much. Day and night I shivered and froze and never really got warm.

I well realized that I was not the only victim subjected to this punishment, as there may have been others even worse off than I was. The new year, 1940, had its first sunrise: the

(Top left) Salween Bridge toward the Tibet border.

(Top right) Fr. Burdin, P.F.M. The "Flying Horse" preferred land...

Tibet caravans leave Tali for the snowy trails of the hump.

Tibetan hunter and dog, as forbidding as Tibet.

(Top) Tibetan steppes country 30 days from Tali to Yerkalo.

Meekong River and the Burma Road. Wheels were salvaged for horse carts...

Reverse Lend-Lease from warphan. Toishan voted him a testimonial banner...

Tibetan solitude. Long-haired yaks graze in the valley primeval. Marco Polo called them wondrous to behold.

Solid silver adorns the women. Square amulet every Tibetan wears holds magic pills, mystic prayers, tiny idols and Living Buddha's whiskers.

Author, Bishop Walsh, General-issimo Chiang, Fr. Smith, Mr. Yeh. Chiang said, "Missioners coming will be most welcome"...

The Quads or Double Twins. The mother cried; she saved confinement fees for only one...

Without a rudder.
Flood brought youngsters on anything that would float.

Yellow River flood ravaged cities. A man was tried for selling human flesh.

Sampan over the flood. Tears did not dry with the flood waters ...

Village near Chung-king where beauty runs in curves.

Refugees found the missioners pillars of support.

Chair bearers on Kiangsi trails. Reds were ousted in 1935.

Summer style is apron and orchids.

Toishan warphans. Fr. O'Neill fed 1000 daily in his rice line.

Fourteenth sends a bomber. St. Paul's Captain Ted Michael swung Topong Mission into his bombsight. "Release at count of three," he ordered.

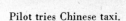

Pilot tries Chinese taxi.

The bomber's hum startled Fr. McLaughlin. Captain Michael spotted his flaming red hair...

Fr. Dempsey got out, hiked six days to Liuchow. The gunmen apologized to him...

Flight of the refugees. No one
asked, "Is this trip necessary?"

The Jolly Roman an
G.I. friends. Gen. Chei
nault took his arm .

Riding the rods to sa
ty. G.I.'s helped . . .

thought of what the newborn year would bring dominated the minds of many unfortunate victims sitting behind iron bars. None of us would dare promise himself anything. There was nothing to give any indication or foreboding of what to expect. Many, I am sure, were gripped with bitter thoughts and miserable despair.

New Year's Day was marked with a medical inspection. The Russian doctor who examined me declared that my lungs were affected and wrote out a prescription. If I had to wait for the medicine prescribed I should perhaps still be in prison today, for it never came.

More than six successive months, from August to February, were spent in the solitude of that cell. It was leap year, and February was just about to fade out after its twenty-ninth sunset when the Lord was mindful of His unworthy servant behind the bars and had me transferred to another prison, which turned out to be the remodeled dispensary of our Catholic mission.

I deemed myself happy to have arrived once more in the sacred precincts of our former mission compound. Once again, thank God, we had the luxury of wooden floors. Fleas and lice were scarcely noticeable. Wooden planks gave way to straw sacks for beds. The rooms were large and airy and such a contrast to what we had just left that we felt as though we had been lifted at least to the second heaven.

After a few days the Chief of Police and Uglin, the Russian, called for an inspection. When the latter asked how I was faring, to be truthful I had to declare, "Not too well. Malaria is sapping my strength, and acute abdominal pains apparently result from lack of clothing and warm bedding."

The same day a real bed was brought in and fixed up for me. When the doctor called he wrote out a prescription which relieved my suffering a great deal. Furthermore, I received a change of underclothes, permitting me after many, many weeks to have the old ones washed.

Soon after the transfer to the dispensary-prison, I discovered that the Widow Draus and her two daughters were living in a room across the yard. On Easter, a parcel containing some small loaves of raisin bread, together with colored eggs and apples, were sent across the yard by the Draus children. Soon they received permission from the Chief of Police to care for my laundry and to continue to send me articles of food. No one in the world can imagine what this kindness and generosity on the part of those children meant to me.

The month of October was upon us again when orders came to pack up our personal belongings and get ready to travel. Under strong police escort we were led to the main mission station, which likewise had been turned into a prison. Some sixty to seventy prisoners were confined there. Shortly after the transfer to this new "jail" I learned of the presence of Father Oirschot in the neighboring room. Soon we succeeded in exchanging communications. Caught in the act, I was punished by a transfer to another room, bare of all furnishings. I had to sleep on the floor.

Finally, on January 2, 1941, a police officer arrived and ordered me to pack up my few articles quickly. He hurried me off to an auto waiting in the yard, told me to climb in and to lie down flat. A few moments later Father Oirschot arrived and was ordered to do likewise. A large canvas was thrown over us. Evidently it was intended to keep the populace from knowing what was happening to us. The auto rumbled through the town and pulled in at the Police Headquarters. From a large pile of clothing we were asked to pick out our own belongings and bundle them in a sack.

"You will now go to Tihwa," we were told. In surprise we asked, "How about the clothing and other articles that were taken from us when we were first arrested a year and a half ago?"

"All that belongs to you," they said, "will be returned later on." But the promise was never fulfilled.

The day was bitter cold. Iron chains were fastened about our legs. We lay on the truck like two pigs being hauled to market. Sorrowfully we realized that we were losing much of church property and of our personal belongings. But, thank God, we were still alive, and in our gratitude could forget the biting cold and the bouncing, rolling back and forth on the wooden floor of the truck.

We reached Tihwa on the fourth of January. There we spent another four days in prison, wondering what fate still had in store for us.

Finally, on the eighth of January, the iron door of the prison cell swung open and with a sweeping gesture the official ordered me to bundle my belongings. As I reached the prison door a dark cloth was thrown over my head. I was led into another room, and my head was uncovered. Shortly afterward Father Oirschot arrived in the same condition. Later, in another room, we came face to face with our confreres, Msgr. Loy and Fathers Hilbrenner and Metter. It was hard to restrain the impulse to weep and to fall into each other's arms. Here we were gathered once more, the five sole survivors of the Sinkiang mission field.

Msgr. Loy and the other two fathers had already been forced to sign away all claim to any movable mission property for the paltry sum of eighty-five hundred Chinese dollars. Father Oirschot and I were likewise requested to sign. When I protested the injustice, the official bluntly declared, "Be prepared to return to prison. The others shall be released to go to Kansu."

Msgr. Loy, my superior, advised me to sign, as a refusal would mean just the same thing so far as the property was concerned but would mean further torture and probable death for me.

That same evening the five of us missionaries who had spent more than ten years in laboring for the souls of Sinkiang found our mission slipping away in the distance as two autos raced us to the border of Kansu and to freedom once more.

III . . . Assault by Man and Nature

1 . . . Curiosities of Chinese Finances

WHEN I ARRIVED in Chungking in February, 1942, it cost thirty-five dollars a day (two dollars in U. S. money) for food. When I left in January, 1945, it cost eight hundred and fifty dollars Chinese and the daily food bill was steadily going up. Chinese currency had less value than German currency after the last war. When the Japanese came close to Chungking in December, 1944, people were offering six hundred dollars in national currency for one American greenback. In April, 1945, they gave eight hundred for the dollar. In June, after the Chinese government had raised the price for gold metal from twenty thousand to thirty-five thousand dollars N.C. an ounce, people were offering twelve to fourteen hundred for one U.S. dollar. During July, buyers in Kunming were paying three thousand Chinese for one American dollar.

With Protestant mission treasurers, I called several times on Dr. H. H. Kung, Minister of Finance, pointing out the necessity of adjusting the exchange to correspond with the rising inflationary prices if mission work were to continue. We realized China was facing a problem without counterpart in Western economic history. One of my Chinese banking friends made this clear when he said, "China is not well organized for a situation like this. The people are not organized and disciplined as in foreign countries and price control cannot be enforced."

When the government promulgated control measures, merchants and traders simply closed up shop and hoarded their goods, rather than sell at fixed prices. The black market became the recognized market—and the government was unable to stamp it out. An absurd situation prevailed: while uncontrolled prices skyrocketed, the exchange for foreign currencies coming in was controlled or fixed. It was fixed by agreement among China, United States and Britain, and people sending funds to China first had to get government permits, then send the funds by bank transfer at the fixed rate. Britain and America refused to allow their citizens to send foreign currency or checks (except for American soldiers) into China. This was disastrous for the missions and others depending on funds from abroad for their work and livelihood.

The Associated Church Treasurers' Offices (for Protestant missions) made a chart for the period from 1937 to April 1, 1945, comparing the rise of exchange and the rise in prices. The price index was from the University of Nanking figures. They conclude from their chart: "If the purchasing value of the U.S. dollar had gone up with the corresponding rise in costs, the American dollar should exchange for [Chinese National Currency] $4,384.52 . . . in March 1945."

The history behind this is worth reviewing. With war draining China's resources from 1937, she was approaching inflation in 1940-41. Her foreign credit balances were fast disappearing as she purchased war materials abroad. The Republic's trade had suffered a staggering blow with the loss of Shanghai to the Japanese in 1937 (Shanghai had been the world's largest port in volume of trade). Most of the Republic's imports had come in through the great harbor at the mouth of the Yangtze, and this had given the government a large income in customs taxes. Before this trade could be shunted, at least in part, to other ports, these, too, fell to the Japanese. By December, 1941, Japan had sealed off the last two routes for trade and delivery of materials to China—Hongkong and Indo-China.

Customs duties and other income from foreign trade were now completely cut off.

In the spring of 1941 Britain and America came to China's help in an attempt to stave off economic ruin. America loaned U.S. $50,000,000 and Britain loaned £10,000,000 to try to stabilize China's currency. The three countries decided to peg the currency as it was then, $18.75 to one U.S. dollar. (A year later the official exchange was still the same, but Lessing Buck, former husband of the writer Pearl Buck, calculated that the actual value of the American dollar was then $350 N.C. instead of $18.75.) The Stabilization Board of China was formed with one American member, one British and three Chinese.

Chairman of the Stabilization Board was the affable K. P. Chen, head of the big Shanghai Commercial and Savings Bank. Mr. Sol Adler was the American member, Mr. Hall-Patch the British, and the two remaining members were K. K. Kwok and Pei Tsu-yi, heads of the Central Bank and Bank of China respectively.

Although K. P. Chen speaks and writes English fluently, he always conversed with me in Chinese. I learned a great deal about economics and banking from his sane, intelligent comments. Mr. Chen has the reputation of believing in private enterprise rather than government monopolies.

Mr. Sol Adler, who succeeded Mr. Fox as American member, is a likable, kindly man. Many of the Chinese commented that he was a good economist, but less outstanding on finance. They called him a theorist, not a practical economist. Sol was most sympathetic and understanding about the difficulties of those depending on funds from abroad and handicapped by the pegged exchange.

Hall-Patch was a good Scottish finance man who had been bank and finance adviser in Burma for many years. He was blunt and honest, and he could put economic theories and facts in a way that made sense to a common man.

Kwok and Pei were both capable bankers, but K. K. Kwok was more approachable and helpful. Many of us in Chungking found the two banks reflections of the men heading them: the Bank of China was strictly business; the Central Bank was business with helpful service.

With the loans from Britain and the United States, the Board set up a stabilization fund and bought heavily when Chinese currency weakened. But this artificial breather was not enough. China, behind a blockade, had goods to sell without a market—and nobody is rich with either goods or money if he cannot use them. So the currency went on losing value apace. The government had little income from trade or business, and naturally Dr. Kung could not balance the budget. Then the government printed a flood of currency without any backing except faith in the country itself, and faith in the country weakened as the Japanese took over more and more territory. Bankers and finance men were losing confidence as the government poured more paper currency off the presses each month. Hundred-dollar bills were issued in great quantities. Then, later, two-hundred-dollar bills were released. In 1944, five-hundred-dollar and one-thousand-dollar bills appeared.

Dr. H. H. Kung, Minister of Finance, was easily approached on the hardships the low exchange rate was causing, but because of many problems involved he held off on making adjustment. This descendant of Confucius (Kung Fu-tze), now in his sixties, had had his ups and downs in the political battles of a long career and knew how to give and take. One day at lunch with him, he told me why he had become a Christian. Although a great advocate of the Confucian doctrine of ethics, he said, he found in his studies as a young man that "Christianity is the necessary completion of Confucianism. Confucius taught virtue for virtue's sake only, without the view of after life that Christ brought."

Dr. Kung went to the Protestant Yenching University and became a Protestant. "Do you know," he said, "there are almost one million Protestants in China. How many Catholics are there?" I told him upward of three and a half million and he looked astonished.

Mme. Kung, sister of Mme. Chiang Kai-shek and of Finance Minister T. V. Soong, also turned out to be a clever and delightful personality. She, too, had considerable influence. With inflation prices forcing our Maryknoll Leper Colony toward closure, I once rang her doorbell to ask a favor: if we could get military or government rice at the low fixed price (the price fixed when the rice was taken in as taxes), the colony could survive. Mme. Kung wrote the Kwangtung governor's wife, and in a matter of days Father Sweeney, in charge of the colony, received a letter informing him that he could obtain the rice at the low government price—"at cost." At the same time, Dr. Kung himself made a generous donation to the colony.

In spite of all pleading and protest, Dr. Kung fought off adjusting the exchange all through 1942-43 because it was to China's advantage to let the rate stand. The United States was spending thirty million dollars U.S. a month putting in air bases. In round figures, America was getting twenty dollars N.C. for one dollar U.S., when she should have been getting two hundred dollars Chinese to correspond with inflationary costs. The army paid coolies one hundred dollars (five dollars U.S. and up) a day on the base construction jobs. It is simple arithmetic to see that China was getting thirty million U.S. dollars in foreign credit instead of the three million she would have got if the exchange had been realistically adjusted.

True, China's economy was so shaky that an increased exchange rate might have hastened collapse—and America needed to keep China in the war and would pay a big price to do it. But political figures in the administration at Washington feared Congress might demand an inquiry into our apparent extravagance in China, and so every effort was made to prevail on Chungking to make an adjustment.

Those who pressed for this were our Ambassador, Clarence Gauss, and the American and British members of the stabilization board—Sol Adler and Mr. Hall-Patch.

This was the situation of fixed exchange and inflation prices when the United States Army started coming in numbers late in 1942. General Stilwell, taking a realistic view, gave his soldiers their pay in American currency. Treasury officials wished to have this stopped, but Stilwell made a detailed report to General Marshall at Washington, who decided in favor of Vinegar Joe's financial policy: G.I.'s could sell their greenbacks on the street at a high rate and thus get a more proportionate value for their dollar. The United States Treasury resented this move of the Army but could not do much about it.

Next, President Roosevelt sent Ted Acheson, brother of Undersecretary of State Dean Acheson, to see what he could do about the exchange rate in Chungking. Ted had been in North Africa and in England, arranging lend-lease agreements. He arrived with letters from Mr. Roosevelt accrediting him as representing not only the War and Treasury Departments but the President himself. He promptly went into the arena with Dr. Kung, and the sparring lasted for months.

Acheson had a sharp mind and was a clever talker and a correct diplomat at the same time. A few days after his arrival I met him at a dinner given by General Thomas Hearn, Chief-of-Staff to General Stilwell, and I visited him every week during the prolonged period of his negotiations with Dr. Kung and the Generalissimo. Fortunately for our work, Ted took on the task of softening up Dr. Kung on behalf of the missions as well as on behalf of the government. After considerable pressure, Dr. Kung agreed that the mission societies could sell frozen credits in America to Chinese or others on the open market. It would not be official recognition, but he gave us his blessing to go ahead.

Catholic and Protestant societies set up a joint clearing board in Chungking to sell credits deposited in the National City Bank in New York. The Chinese business firms bought United States currency credit for, say, $100,000 and paid the clearing board in Chinese N.C. at the exchange rate fixed by the board. The rate varied with the open-market rate of United States currency. The Chinese firm got a frozen credit deposited with National City for purchases in America, and the board received Chinese currency for mission and relief uses. Thus, after more than two years' difficulties with fixed exchange vs. inflation, the missions were at last able to get a fairer value for the subsidies from home.

In January, 1944, Dr. Kung finally admitted to Acheson that there should be a general adjustment of the exchange rate, but he kept delaying action. Since, however, he had admitted the principle, Acheson suggested, "While you deliberate on the new rate, let us draw Chinese currency for construction of air bases and other American army needs. Then, when the new rate goes into effect, we can figure the gold credit China gets in America."

Dr. Kung agreed to this and all saved faces. The official rate of exchange never has been altered—it was to be decided at a later settlement. But the danger of an embarrassing investigation—and of the American public complaining of being taken in at a rate of twenty to one—was averted. Acheson had won his point.

The settlement was made in January, 1945. Here is the treasury department press release of January 22.

"The U.S. Treasury Department has just completed transfer to the Republic of China of $210,000,000 in settlement for advances of local currency and for supplies, services and military construction furnished the U.S. Forces in China.

"A portion of the settlement came from U.S. funds already in China, a portion from funds previously placed to China's credit in the United States and the remainder in the form of a check for approximately $150,000,000 which Secretary Morgenthau gave to Dr. H. H. Kung here."

I learned unofficially that the exchange rate in the settlement was $120 Chinese National Currency for one U.S. dollar. Officially the twenty-to-one rate stands on the records, but a more practical and realistic rate was agreed upon for the settlement.

2 . . . Missioners as Chaplains

ONE DAY EARLY IN 1944, in the poor and hilly country back of
Kukong, a peasant youth trudging to market with a load of
produce noticed a peculiar white patch on the side of a hill
along the road. Then he saw what appeared to be a man, blue
from head to foot, sitting up there waving. He overcame his
apprehension and went nearer until he perceived that the blue
man was not a Japanese and that he seemed to be in pain.

The Chinese peasant had never before seen such a creature
—almost a boy, with a long nose, hair the color of wet straw
and a reddish skin, wearing a uniform of the color of the sky
and making unintelligible sounds. Near by a shroud of dazzling
white silk lay draped on the bushes. The blue man kept pointing at his left ankle, and the peasant, recognizing that he was
wounded, lifted him onto his sturdy shoulders and plodded
several miles to a village. Here the elders, who were better
informed, saw that the farmer had brought in an American
aviator, an "angel man," wearing a high-altitude heater-suit,
who had come down in a parachute. But what to do with him?
The flier himself solved their problem by producing a pocket
dictionary, pointing to the Chinese characters for Catholic mission. And so a few hours later the young bombardier was
brought to Father Joseph Regan, a Maryknoll missioner from
Fall River, Mass., who doctored his fractured ankle and arranged for his safe return to his base.

Missioners in many parts of China found themselves called
upon to perform such helpful acts as more and more Americans

appeared in this theater of war. A number of them, indeed,
had been serving with the armed forces for some time. Late
in the summer of 1942, Colonel Alexander, chief of the Army's
air office in Chungking, had asked me to stop in at USAAF
headquarters and shown me a pile of messages on his desk.

"All these," he said, "are asking for Catholic chaplains.
It will take months for army chaplains to come out from
the States, and there is a shortage, anyhow. We hoped you
might be able to arrange it so missioners who have been driven
out of their districts by the Japanese could come to work at
the various bases as contract chaplains."

A contract chaplain is a civilian clergyman employed under
contract to serve in the Army, though he is not inducted into
the Army. I was then contract chaplain at Chungking. (Later,
when numbers of regular Army chaplains arrived, Archbishop
Spellman named Bishop Jantzen Military Vicar Delegate to
the armed forces, with myself as his assistant and field worker.)

The problem was this. Groups of American forces were
being stationed at scattered points throughout China—from the
Burma border through snow-mantled peaks and jungle valleys
and east to the Japanese-occupied China coast, and from trop-
ical Indo-China to the frozen regions of the Communist area
in China's Northwest. Their spiritual and often their material
needs were being taken care of by missioners, provided there
was a mission near their post and its incumbent could speak
English. But many of the fathers were Europeans; they could
neither hear G.I. confessions nor act as interpreters for them
with the local inhabitants (of great importance in those many
places where our troops had to shift for themselves by trading
with the natives).

"Our men are fighting and being shot down," went on
Colonel Alexander, "and we must have someone on hand to
take care of their religious needs. We would like to have a
contract chaplain in Kunming immediately, for instance."

Fortunately, a priest was available. Father Edward Lyons, Canadian Scarboro missioner, who had been driven out of Chekiang and who was with me in Chungking, left by plane at eight the next morning, rejoicing in this opportunity to serve. During the next eighteen months we were able to "lend" the army a score more of priests who had been dispossessed by the enemy.

General Chennault sent me a letter expressing his appreciation for the kind services of missioners for the American boys in China. It is quoted here in part:

"Here in China owing to difficulties of wide dispersal and inadequate transportation it would have been impossible for the fine body of commissioned Chaplains belonging to the Fourteenth Air Force to provide adequately for the religious needs of all our men. Here the Missionaries stepped in. With the arrival of the first troops on a new base the Missionaries made their presence felt, providing religious services, guiding, counselling—and offering their homes as another home for these splendid but often lonely soldiers of ours.

"In some cases where this was not enough, they devoted their full time to caring for our troops as Civilian Contract Chaplains. Their work in this country will not soon be forgotten by the men they served.

"Men forced down at great distance from any of our bases have time and again been rescued by nearby Missionaries and have found a home and care until they could be returned to their organizations.

"In fact everywhere they might help they offered themselves, remembering always that they were men of God and never entering into any activity which might contradict that status. Nevertheless when the story of the victory of the forces of Right against a barbaric enemy is written, theirs will be an important chapter. Seeking only to serve God and their fellow men they have been a source of inspiration, of encouragement, of strength to all of us.

"Respectfully yours,

C. L. Chennault

"Major General, U.S.A. Commanding."

The missioners took to army life naturally, since they had served under conditions of danger and privation for years; many had marched for weeks and months with the retreating Chinese. I remember later visiting Father Morrell, an army chaplain from St. Louis, at a military post in the highlands on the Burma border. He lived in a tent near a hospital hidden in a deep ravine. After shivering all night with all my clothes on under six blankets, and washing with icy water in a steel helmet in the morning, I told him he could now have a fair idea of what a missioner's life was like.

I saw chaplains saying Mass in hangars, in tents, on the hoods of jeeps. At one post the G.I.'s hammered candlesticks from the aluminum of a crashed plane and altered and painted an oil drum to make a tabernacle. One of the boys brought in a used parachute, and sisters at a near-by convent made it into vestments for Mass. "To us these vestments were more resplendent than any to be seen in the windows of New York City's Church Row on Barclay Street," said the chaplain.

In 1944, Father Joseph Cosgrove of Maryknoll had been a contract chaplain with fighter squadrons for three years. He was always at an advanced base, and the men claimed he had had more bombs fall around him than any other priest. When he was sent to a rear base for a respite he at once complained and was sent right back. The men gathered on the field to cheer him when he returned, for he had become an integral part of their work; in addition to bringing them the comfort of religion he was used for material tasks because of his knowledge of Chinese. He got information from country folk when he went out with groups looking for downed planes, and he successfully dickered with local militia for surviving Japanese aviators that American officers wanted to question. When there was sufficient time, he conducted evening classes in Chinese.

Father Cosgrove was cited for his aid to crashed fliers. He was noted for the speed with which he reached our planes when they landed on the field crippled or blazing. He had received a commendation from the commanding officer for dashing into a burning plane and pulling out its occupants while the machine-gun ammunition was exploding in every direction.

Ammunition exploding on a burning plane is a frightening thing to witness. I saw it happen on the field at Kunming, where I went on a tour of duty in the spring of 1943. This, incidentally, was the first time I witnessed something much more memorable—Japanese planes in rout, defeated by our P-40's. Up to that time I had seen them come over Wuchow and other places a score of times, dropping their bombs at will.

It was a fine May morning. I looked out of my window and saw a red ball going up on the pole at the airfield a mile away. That, I knew, meant "enemy coming this way." A second red ball went up—"enemy approaching"—and then the sirens started screaming. I hurried to the street, where the people were running in every direction, chiefly toward open spaces and out toward the airport.

The road out of town was a stream of clamorous humanity, most of the people running barefoot, but some riding in rickety two-wheeled carts drawn by chunky little horses from the Yunnan hills. These carts were rubber-tired, mostly with American tires taken from supply trucks wrecked on the hairpin turns of the Burma Road.

Near the airport I saw some American boys in a slit trench and dived in beside them, while shark-nosed P-40's went roaring up to support a reconnaissance squadron that had located the enemy. The men said sixty to seventy Japanese planes were headed this way. Pretty soon we saw a cloud of planes in the sky—Japanese bombers, forging steadily ahead like killer whales, thirty-six of them by count; playing in and out among them like fierce protecting barracudas were about forty fast little Zeros; and zooming high and then diving down through the enemy formations were our own P-40 sharks, less maneuverable than the Zeros but faster and deadlier.

As the Japanese drew close, a mass dive-attack by the P-40's threw the bombers off their aim, and their deadly eggs plowed up the countryside beyond the base. But a few small bombs fell on the edge of the field and fragments set fire to a parked B-24. We cheered when the first Zero came smoking down and crashed with a terrific explosion on a hill a few miles away. The frustrated bombers turned and fled, with the P-40's on their tails; the battle moved out of sight and hearing, and we were jubilantly filing out of our slit trench when the ammunition started exploding on the burning B-24, the bullets flying in every direction.

As American air activity was stepped up in 1944, fliers returning in crippled planes often had to bail out over wild, isolated parts of the country, where backward or uninformed inhabitants were more suspicious than hospitable. Many an American lad has been saved uncomfortable moments, and perhaps something worse, by the prompt arrival of a missioner who got word that a man had dropped out of the sky. "Fah-thah, I cahn't make them understand," a flier from Massachusetts would tell the priest; or "How you min all doin'?" would ask a lad from Carolina; or the Southern Californian would quip, "This here cain't compare with the climate we got at home."

Sometimes it wasn't simple for the missioner to reach the flier. Father James O'Day, from Providence, R. I., woke up at 1:30 A. M. on May 20, 1944, to hear the sounds of a violent thunderstorm, his dogs barking and a rapping on his door. Two Chinese had come to the Maryknoll Mission—this was in North Kwangtung province, in coastal country not occupied by the Japanese—to inform him that American aviators had come down fifteen miles away. One had landed in a ricefield and was recovering in a Christian farmer's house.

Father O'Day took along a can of coffee in his old motorcycle which had a sidecar, only to learn that the storm had washed a fifteen-foot gap in the road. He wanted to bring the flier back in the sidecar but knew he couldn't make it with the machine in the dark, so he waited until dawn. Then he fought soupy mud for six hours before reaching his destination, where they told him the American had gone out in search of a buddy. A few minutes later a strange procession appeared: first a group of excited farmers, then four men carrying a chair slung on two poles, with a bleeding American lad in the chair, then another flier, who seemed dazed. The last, when he saw the priest, stopped in his tracks and asked, "Are you a white man?" When he heard Father O'Day's unmistakable New England accent he almost wept.

One by one the crew members of the abandoned Liberator were located and brought together by Father O'Day, who gave first aid to the wounded and managed to scare up bread, jam and other items of food that set better with the fliers than the unaccustomed Chinese rice. Soon he had them in good shape and en route to an army base.

If the missioners thus aided American fighting men, these in turn were quite often able to help the priests and sisters and their Chinese people. G.I.'s who saw Father Edmund J. McCabe swamped by refugee work raised a fund for him at his post in Chuanchow, near Hengyang, when the Japanese were pushing down from Changsha in the first phase of their

1944 offensive. Others who heard of his plight through Theater Chaplain McNamara also made a collection for him.

When the day came to pull out of Chuanchow, Father McCabe began to worry over two Chinese Maryknoll nuns who had insisted on remaining at their dangerous post. He found that the trains passing through were filled to capacity with refugees from the north, but he was an obstinate man and stayed around the station. And sure enough, the next day a group of G.I's stepped off a train that had just come in and said, "Father, can you speak this language? We're hungry but we can't talk Chinese."

While Father McCabe took care of them they told him they had loaded up a train at Hengyang but couldn't find an engineer—military trains draw enemy bombers. One of the soldiers, however, knew how to run a locomotive. And so here they were on their way to Kweilin; they had stopped because they were hungry. When Father McCabe told them about the two Chinese sisters, their spokesman stated, "Father, no one will start this so-and-so train until they are on. You just go back and get them, we'll be here." Father Cosgrove had been their chaplain up the line, he explained—"and this is the least we can do to repay what he done for us."

Father McCabe dashed back to the mission, where the faithful sisters delayed matters by arguing that they should remain with him. Finally a sergeant came for them in a weapons carrier, and by the time they got back to the station the G.I. engineer was at his post tooting the whistle.

"The station master was tearing his hair," he said. "He wanted us to get out of the way. Well, we told him, 'You got to sweat it out, feller, until they get here.'" The station master was still tearing his hair, but when he saw the sisters he grinned and helped find them a place.

Forty-eight hours later, Japanese tanks came in sight of the town. At the last moment, a jeep full of soldiers came by and took Father McCabe to safety.

3 . . . The Fourteenth Sends a Bomber

On Friday, October 13, 1944, a Mitchell bomber of China's air force circled over a clearing in the Kwangsi mountains. Ripening grain carpeted the terraced rice paddies. Clusters of mud-walled homes marked a village of farmers who worked the fields. The pilot strained his eyes, searching for a hideout where eight missioners fleeing ahead of an enemy army had concealed themselves. This pilot was on an unprecedented mission, a task that no airman in the Fourteenth had ever undertaken.

When he sighted his objective he buzzed low, skimming over a tower and a cross. Chickens scattered, dogs scampered and frightened children fell flat on the ground, to escape the plane that came swooping down on them. The fliers had a package to deliver, but they must be sure it fell into the hands of the American missioners who had taken refuge in the mountains after being driven out of the plains below. The pilot banked his plane inside the encircling peaks to discover an American. The men he looked for had seen the star and the bar on his plane, emblem of the American air force, and they came out. Captain Michael saw the flaming red hair on one of the men. He was sure now that the American priests were still there, so he prepared to complete his mission.

The group of cornered men in hiding below were there because of the Japanese push in mid-September. The armies had swept up the West River from Canton. It was a wide sweep that overran all the towns and cities for forty miles each side of the river, to insure their advance. As the enemy soldiers drew close to each Maryknoll mission along the West River, the priests skipped out to avoid capture. When they came to Wuchow, first city in Kwangsi province, Bishop Frederick Donaghy of Fall River and Father Peter Reilly of Boston cleared out for a near-by mountain village just beyond reach. They hoped the enemy would pass on through and they could come back to aid the ravaged city.

About eighty miles upstream from Wuchow is Pingnam. It was prearranged that all the men on or near the West River, at places above and below Pingnam, would gather there when the enemy started up river. From Pingnam they would make for a village called Topong in the deep fastnesses of the mountains, and there they would go into hiding. They hoped this would be safe because it was difficult to approach and offered no military advantage or lure of booty to the invading soldiers.

Zero day had arrived and the Japanese came smashing into deserted Wuchow. They continued their advance up river, swallowing the missions of Yunghui, Tangyuen and Tanchuk. But they found at each place that the American missioners had just departed for Pingnam and the mountains.

Fifty miles up from the Pingnam cutoff to the hideout were two other missions and a seminary. A telegram told them they must start down quickly, to make Pingnam ahead of the Japanese. Father Albert Fedders of Louisville, Kentucky, and Father Cyril Hirst of Philadelphia hired a boat with six oarsmen to make a rush for it. They were heading toward machine guns and it was a race against time, for the Japanese were marching up the river and might get to Pingnam first. With the promise of a large bonus, and with nagging, cajoling and encouraging, the two worried priests got the boatmen to row day and night. The oars creaked, the rowers sweated and cursed, but they won the race and got to Pingnam a day before the Japanese. At Pingnam they joined up with the other priests hiking across the plain toward the trail that led into the mountain hideout of Topong. Next day the Japanese came into Pingnam, but the American priests were gone again.

After hiking all day they arrived at the edge of the plain, stopping overnight at the mission of Szewong with Father Paul Welty of Martinsburg, West Virginia. All except Father Welty started up the mountain trail early next morning. He decided to stay another day in his mission of Szewong, since the Japanese were only then marching into Pingnam, fifteen miles away. Toward evening the people in the town of Szewong became frightened. Rumor said the Japanese would close in on the town that night.

Father Welty packed a bag and went to the little Christian village of Ha Lo, three miles away, to pass the night. It was a lucky move, for at three o'clock next morning two hundred Japanese drove into the town of Szewong. They pounded on the mission gate until it was opened; then they tied up the gatekeeper, trying to force him to tell where the American resident had gone. All he revealed was that the priest had gone the night before, no one could say where.

A runner from the town groped through the night to Ha Lo to warn Father Welty. He dashed off before dawn toward the trail into the mountains. As he climbed he could hear the Japanese machine-gun fire in the villages below. It was a near miss, but no one was caught and all were safely winding their way to the hideout.

The trail was a dangerous path along a river that jumped down over sheer rock cliffs; it was too narrow to enter even on horseback.

Where the trail finished its climb, far away in the little valleys between high mountains, the people had terraced the land into rice paddies and villages had grown up. Many of the villagers had become Christian; the region was so difficult of access that the mission of Topong was built in the heart of the district and a priest sent there to live. The mission was built fifteen years ago by Father Meyer, who was a prisoner of the Japanese at Hongkong throughout the war.

In Topong the eight American missioners were cut off not only from the Japanese but from funds and friends. They held council and decided to send a runner out the back way and over higher mountains with a letter to the air base chaplain at Liuchow. The letter asked him to get in touch with me at Chungking to see if funds could be quickly flown back by plane to Liuchow.

A few days after the runner left, Father Arthur Dempsey of Peekskill, New York, and three companions started scaling the mountains over the back trail toward the air base. For four days they tramped over the mountains, the hardest climbing Father Dempsey had known in his fifteen years in China. With every mile through this savage country, he had misgivings about his return. This is the land of the Yaos, descendants of Chinese aborigines who found sanctuary up here when invading soldiers from the north overran the fertile subtropical valleys two thousand years ago. No white man had ever penetrated this miniature Tibet, whose people are hardy hunters and fierce fighters.

On the second day, as Father Dempsey approached Luk Ngoh (Six Geese Village) in the heart of the Yao mountains, he was met by "five of the roughest-looking individuals this side of Texas." All carried old-fashioned rifles, and they were distinguished by "dark Indian skin, braided black hair tied in a bun atop their heads, with rings, bracelets and trinkets all over their persons, in their ear lobes, on their wrists, fingers and ankles." The five hunters cocked their rifles and demanded to examine the party's baggage. They apologized when they found that Father Dempsey was from the mission at Topong, where they had gone several times for medicine. They invited him to pass the night in their village. The people of Six Geese

Village turned out to be very friendly and gave the travelers a supper of rice, eggs, chicken and squash.

No one knows exactly how high the Yao mountains are. One stretch of seventeen miles took eight hours, "during which the sun shone only for thirty minutes." Father Dempsey and his companions had to cross so many torrents that they gave up their heavy footwear and used woven grass shoes.

On the fourth day out, the little party came to a stream that flows into Liuchow, and they were lucky enough to find a sampan manned by experts at shooting rapids. They reached their destination after two days of thrills and near spills.

One morning in October, four dusty, bedraggled fellows appeared on the Liuchow airfield, where Captain Michael and a crew of the Fourteenth Air Force were tinkering with a bomber's new engines.

"Where is the chaplain?" asked Father Dempsey.

"I'll take you there," offered Captain Michael.

The chaplain had good news. The money had arrived from Chungking. When the fliers asked Father Dempsey how he intended delivering the funds, he said, "We'll hike back the way we came," adding, "unless you fellows drop me down in a parachute!"

Captain Michael thought this over. "I don't like those so-called hunters you told about," he said. "Anyway, I just got new engines in the bomber and I have to do some slow-timing to break them in. Could you point out the mission house from the air, do you think?"

"Sure," said Father Dempsey.

"Well, we'll take you over and drop the money."

"I'm your navigator!" cried Father Dempsey, enthusiastically. "When do we start?"

"Right now."

The currency from Chungking, enough to keep the beleaguered missioners in food for a year, was tightly wrapped in cloth, then placed in a round wicker basket and wedged in solidly with straw.

The Mitchell bomber flew down the West River until Father Dempsey could see the Pingnam plain, on which little black feathers of smoke rose from Maryknoll missions now occupied by the Japanese. Then the plane turned toward the mountains. As it headed in between the peaks, over the chasm trail which the refugees had climbed a week before, Captain Michael asked if the priest was still sure of his directions.

Father Dempsey shouted in his ear, "I know this country like my prayers! Eagle Beak Cliff is up at the end of the pass. You take the left branch of the stream there, hop over one more range and you'll see the valley with the mission. You are right on the beam."

The bomber went on, weaving its way between the peaks, and suddenly the whitewashed mud walls of the mission gleamed below.

"There's your target," shouted Father Dempsey. Then he went back to hold onto the crew chief, who stood over the open hatch with the basket of money.

On the second buzz over the house, the priests who had recognized the insignia came out and waved at the circling plane. The third run was to be a low swoop and the money was to be released at the count of three. The crew chief bent over the hatch, his belt gripped by Father Dempsey and the radio man. Captain Michael was giving signals with his fingers— "One . . . two . . . three!"—and the basket went tumbling two hundred feet toward the mission. It was a bull's-eye: the basket bounced smack in front of the door.

The bomber once more dipped low and banked over the mission. The red-headed Father John McLaughlin of Elmhurst, Long Island, had picked up the basket and stood in front of the door smiling and waving. Captain Michael happily waved back.

When I told General Chennault's chief of staff, General Glynn, about this successful air-drop, he told me that he would be glad to provide us with a bomber when a plane was needed to drop food or medicine to the men at Topong.

Hardly more than a month later, the Japanese took the airfield at Liuchow and also occupied Kweilin, thus completely isolating our people in the Topong mountains. We had no news of them for seven months, but we knew they were provided for and doubted that the Japanese would bother their eyrie. We worried more about Bishop Donaghy and Father Reilly, who hadn't been heard from since their flight from Wuchow. One of many wild rumors that reached us said they had been captured. All we knew was that they had headed up the Foo Valley and at last reports they had been seen in Muk-pon-long, a village some fifteen miles from Wuchow.

In April, 1945, a runner who risked his life passing through the enemy lines arrived in Chungking from Topong. It was the first word from the priests since the bomber dropped their funds six months before. The letter stated that the two missioners from Wuchow were safe in the mountain hideout. On the way from Wuchow they had lived first in one village, then in another, and had walked a hundred and fifty miles, following mountain paths around the towns occupied by the Japanese. They will have a great story to tell when they return from the land of the Yaos.

It was not long before we were to take advantage of General Glynn's offer to drop supplies to cutoff missioners. Messages came through from the coast at Yeungkong behind Japanese lines. They pleaded for urgently needed supplies, clothes and medicines. Setting out at once, the relief plane developed engine trouble one hundred and fifty miles from Yeungkong and was forced to jettison the cargo. The plane came back on one engine and the priests wrote off the attempt as a total loss.

A short time later a runner brought a letter to Chungking

from Father Joseph McGinn, stationed at Kochow, some distance from Yeungkong. He wrote a letter of thanks for "the manna from heaven." He had found on his grounds the supplies for isolated missioners and not knowing they were jettisoned, wrote, "What is the matter, doesn't the American army use parachutes for dropping supplies any more?"

This will be remembered as the miracle of Yeungkong, for the sorely-needed supplies destined for Yeungkong were jettisoned at a point one hundred and fifty miles from there, landing in the yard of the Kochow mission, from which they finally reached Yeungkong.

4 . . . Flight over Everest

DURING MY STAY in Chungking, mission business sent me
several times to India, and I flew over the Hump nine times
in all. Most of my visits were brief and restricted to places in
eastern India, but on one trip I flew all the way to the Red
Sea and skirted the length of the Himalayas, behind which lies
Tibet, the least known part of this inhabited globe.

On this journey I saw the roofs of missions right on the
borders of the Forbidden Land, weeks' travel from any town,
and obtained details about the only white man who lives inside
Tibet (excluding the British commissioner who stays at Lhasa
part of each year). The modern hermit is a French Catholic
missioner.

The bomber in which I flew took off from the plains of
western Szechwan and headed over the China-Tibet border
country toward Kunming. Cruising at about ten thousand feet,
with only now and then a cloud between us and the chaos of
mountains below, we watched the wild country to the west.

In the mountain cities and villages below, French missioners worked among the people of the Tibet border country.
A hundred years ago Tibet mission work was assigned to the
Paris Foreign Mission Fathers, because it was thought more
accessible from west China where they were working. For
almost a hundred years they have been knocking at the gates,
often getting inside the land of mystery, almost as often being
pitched out. In 1857 Bishop Desnazures was appointed for
Lhasa, but he never got there.

In one of the recurrent border wars, the Chinese Army
pushed the Tibetan frontier back many hundred miles, and
Catholic missioners established posts along the new border.
One of these was at Tsakha, more often called Yerkalo. Later
the Tibetans took back the lost territory, but the little mission
had so incorporated itself into the community that it was permitted to remain. It had its ups and downs and the missioners
there had their ins and outs as periodic persecutions swept
across the district. In 1877 there were five hundred Christians
inside Tibet. At the beginning of this century there were 1270.
These converts were bought at a high price, for many a missioner paid with his life. The beginning of this century was
the worst period for the missions. Father Brieux was killed on
the banks of the Blue River near Batang: the lamas, after the
Younghusband expedition of 1904, claimed that he had invited the British to invade their country. Father Mossot was
caught at the mission of Lentzy, tied to a pillar, beaten and
eventually killed. Lamas pursued and caught Father Soule in
the Blue River country. They stripped him, beat him with
thorn bushes and shot him. Other priests along the border
were shot with poisoned arrows, and scores of converts were
massacred.

As the big American plane lurched, bumping, through
clouds on its way to Kunming, I saw a tower and cross standing over a tiny border village. An American explorer once
stopped at this mission on his way to Tibet. He browsed
through the library of Latin, Greek, French and English books,
then said to the priest, "I am not a Catholic, but I'm army
trained and know the value of obedience. What I admire about
your church is that it can plant men like yourself to live on the
last frontier of the world and they go and stay."

After a brief halt at Kunming, we took off again to leap
over the Hump into India. With peaks that jut to fourteen

thousand feet, these mountains run out of Tibet and divide the
Mekong, the Salween and the Irrawaddy. The pilot and co-
pilot kept leaning forward to scan the skies for possible Japanese pursuit. Below was dense wooded jungle, and the mountains were an unbroken carpet of foliage. The mountains here
always have a mantle of protective clouds, the pilot said, and
even if a Zero fighter were sighted we could duck into a cloud
bank and lose him. I hoped so, but kept my eye on the parachute. A cloud bank at sixteen thousand feet put ice on the
antenna and traces on the wings. We climbed above the cloud
layer to twenty-three thousand feet and found white below and
blue above. The pilot spoke of the crew whose plane iced up
and lost so much altitude they had to bail out into the wilder-
ness. After twenty-four days of wandering they came to a village, where their signal was seen by a shuttling transport.
With a water buffalo and a plow they leveled the rice fields
for an emergency field. Then a small trainer plane came and
took them out one at a time. I was glad when, after a few
hours, we got away from the mountains and dropped to the
balmy air over the tea plantations of northeast India. At
Chabua I was billeted with youngsters who talked dreamily
of their homes "in the good old U.S.A."

Up at four-thirty, we were off at six toward Allahabad, New
Delhi and Karachi. Always on our left were the plain, the
meandering rivers, railroads and civilization; always on our
right were the Himalayas and the land of mystery, forbidden
Tibet.

On this flight I sat in the co-pilot's seat with the earphones
on. The pilot let me take the controls and after a while I said
through the mike, "It is easy enough to sit here in the saddle."

"Yeh, until the old horse takes a notion to buck," said the
pilot. He told me that we would soon get a view of Mount
Everest if the weather was clear.

I asked, "Will we be close enough for a good view?"

He said with a knowing smile, "We are supposed to stay well south of these autonomous lands but sometimes a strong south wind just forces us to drift nearer."

There must have been a south wind, for we saw the stately Everest cloaked in snow, glistening in the sun. It looked like a marble pyramid built by one of the kings of Tibet. As we watched the earth's highest peak drift slowly past, I thought of Father Anthony and Brother Maques, the first Europeans to penetrate into the land of mystery beyond. In 1624 these Portuguese missioners crossed the Himalayas and were well received by the Governor of Tibet, but five years later a revolution forced them to leave. After 1640 they tried again but had to abandon the work. I also thought of Father Penna and the group of Capuchins who went up to Lhasa in 1707. These missioners remained until the Mongols invaded Tibet in 1716 and forced them to flee. They returned, but in 1745 revolution again drove them out.

How many converts they made we do not know, but there is a strange monument to their work. The bell in the entrance of the temple of Lhasa today has engraved upon it the Catholic Te Deum Hymn of St. Ambrose, "We praise Thee, God." Sitting behind the bell, lamas chant their pagan prayers.

We flew to New Delhi and then to Karachi, and here I took a train to Bombay. After a brief visit there I crossed the waist of India by train to Calcutta, where I found a plane for the return to China. Thus I was able to get a brief, kaleidoscopic view of this great land whose destiny seems so uncertain and where movements of political resurgence seem almost paradoxical. Everywhere I went, I was struck by the contrast between the Indians and the Chinese.

In the havoc of war, flood or famine—no matter what misfortune—the Chinese is lively, humorous, eager to be on the go, if only to run for safety. In India I got the impression that even the impulse to run was dead. When I talked to people they looked back at me out of lackluster eyes, inclining the head a little to one side or giving a faint, resigned shrug. I exclude, of course, the educated Hindus. I remember particularly what one of them, a bright young lawyer, told me during a train ride: "Of course the British government is good government and without it we might have chaos. But good government is never a substitute for self-government."

Back in Kunming, I had the good fortune to meet one of the missioners stationed on the Tibetan border. This was Father Bonnemin, who had been living for thirteen years at Kionatong on the Salween River. I spent several evenings with this affable French priest, who spoke no Chinese but only his native tongue and Tibetan. The bright sun on the snows of the high country had injured his eyes, and he had come out for treatment. For six months of the year his mission was snowbound. The Salween was frozen over, the roads were impassable and no mail got through. Father Bonnemin lived off the land. He brewed tea that came in bricks from China and thickened it with yak butter; he ate salted meat and wore furlined clothing a great part of the year. He had never seen his bishop, who is at Tatsienlu on the north border, a month's horseback travel. I asked him about his journey back to Kionatong. He said he could go by auto truck the first hundred miles to Tali; then he would ride a horse for three weeks.

"But," he said, "you will be more interested in hearing about Father Burdin, who works in that mission at Yerkalo, the only one inside Tibet's borders. It is ten days by horse and foot from where I am stationed."

Father Burdin has been at Yerkalo since 1940, when his

predecessor, Father Nussbaum, was killed by bandits. In 1939 he paid Father Nussbaum a visit and kept a record of his journey. This record Father Bonnemin now produced, and I translated the highlights:

We left Kionatong mission, which rests in a deep mountain valley on the banks of a stream that sings day and night as it leaps down to the Salween. I like to think of it as the Valley of the Hermit, where Father Bonnemin lives ten days' walk from the nearest white man.

We set off climbing the narrow trail—two ponies and four men. Around ledges not wide enough for baggage and ponies and over fallen trees the men carried the baggage. Eight hours' climb up river beds, ravines and trails, and we pitched tent near the stream for the night. Next day we made the Solola Pass, altitude twelve thousand feet. The fog rose and gave us a view of the Kawakarbo Glaciers to the northeast and snowy mountains all around. Pilgrims come from Lhasa and all parts of Tibet to worship Kawakarbo, the sacred mountain nineteen thousand feet high.

Down the trail into Songtha, first village inside Tibet, we were stopped by the guard. I told him I wished to see my friend the Chielngo (Magistrate). He lived at Ndjrangun, four hours away, and the guard sent us on under escort. I presented letters and gifts to the Chielngo, who had permitted me to pass three years before. He carefully looked over my gifts and said, "We are old friends. There will be no difficulty for the father going to visit the priest at Yerkalo. I shall write a passport for you to show the two military chiefs on the way and you shall pass untroubled." He also put us up for the night and the next day gave us flour, salt meat and wine for the journey.

We had to cross the river that day on a "bamboo bridge," as bridges are known in Tsarong Province, Tibet. There are two cables of woven bamboo. One rope over the river is used for going and another for returning. The starting end is higher than the finishing terminus. A pulley and a sling to sit in are fixed to the cable. You shove off and go tearing across the swirling rapids, sliding to the other end, or almost there. Weather had started to rot the down cable, and I wondered if we should chance it. A few years ago one of the missioners was drowned when a cable broke. One of the party, heavier than I, made the sign of the Cross and jumped into the sling with a prayer. He made it across and so I followed. But the ponies were pulled across laboriously on the up cable. (A thinner rope is used to bring the slings back to the starting point.)

Next day we came in sight of Lhakhongra (Home of the Divinities). Not far away at Bonga there are some Catholics. The route into Lhakhongra follows the canyon, and it is impossible to go around the military post. I showed the passport given me by the magistrate below, but the soldier took us to his captain. The captain said, "I know the father and his good work and I shall be pleased to give you another letter to help you along the way."

Two hours out we overtook a caravan of about sixty ponies at rest. The owner was a merchant transporting tea to Lhasa. We stopped to chat a while. The merchant asked me, "Would you like to journey to Lhasa with us?"

"Too many formalities even coming this far," I answered.

"You can join my train, but under one condition, that is, cut off your beard." We all laughed as we continued the meal he had set up for us.

The next day I was required to show my passport three times but always permitted to continue. At Tchrana and at Menkong where I passed the night I was entertained by watching the pilgrims at prayers. They paraded around and around the Pagoda, uttering on each of the many beads dangling from their fingers, "*Om Mani Padmay Hum.* O thou Jewel of the Lotus Flower."

By coming near Pagodas I stopped the parade. They gathered around me joking about my red beard. Some said, "He speaks our language. That is funny."

After ten days' journeying we came through a pass that brought the village of Yerkalo and the mission into view. I was going to visit the priest who sees a white man once and sometimes twice a year.

And now it is Father Burdin himself who scarcely ever sees a white man. News of world events that are flashed to us the same day reach him six months later.

5 . . . Honan's Bitter Years

JUST AFTER MY ARRIVAL in Chungking in the spring of 1942, Arnold Vaught, Chairman of the American Advisory Committee of Relief, sat beside me at luncheon in the New Life Movement Center and said, "At the committee meeting yesterday it was unanimously voted to invite you to become a member." Then he gave me a bundle of reports that had just come in from the committee's field men, and urged me to accept. He said, "We want you to represent the Catholics engaged in relief work in different parts of China."

The American Advisory Committee is the best organized group in China for the distribution of aid to flood, famine and war victims. It has a subcommittee in each province, which in turn has small district committees made up of Chinese and Americans of all faiths. In addition, field men sent out from Chungking constantly report to headquarters on the work and needs in the different provinces. In 1942 they were receiving and distributing $60,000 in American money per month. Later the relief expenditures grew much larger. I also became a member of the International Relief Committee, the Catholic Committee and several of the committees for United China Relief. The reports that came in from all parts of the country gave a picture of China's suffering.

In August, 1942, up in Kokonor and Kansu, promising provinces of China's northwest, heavy rains filled the innumerable rivulets, creeks and streams that wind their way into the north-flowing Yellow River. In adjacent Suiyan province, where the river suddenly makes a sharp turn south, the people saw what they had often seen before—a quick rise and fall of the river, so marked that it seemed like a lengthy roller. The Yellow River was in flood again.

At the time of my visit to Lanchow, the flood had already receded. Father Depuyt, a gentle, white-bearded Belgian missioner who had been in these parts of China for forty-one consecutive years, urged me to travel with him through the flood-devastated areas on my way back to Chungking.

I agreed, and we set out for his mission at Ningsia on a sheep-pelt raft like those previously described, except for the luxury of a tent-roof. A Moslem and his son paddled the delicate craft around rocks and down whirling rapids for five days. At wayside restaurants in little towns along the shore we were able to get food, such as it was.

Perched on this floating shell were the quiet Belgian father and the two silent pagans. I thought wistfully back to my trips on the river boats of South China—big, wide-bottomed junks that have as much of a life of their own as the fanciest transoceanic liner. I particularly recalled my last trip, three days up the West River from Wuchow on the way to my assignment in Chungking. I thought of the frequent meals cooked and served aboard; the leisurely hours of being towed up the slothful stream by a wheezing steam launch; the fakirs and salesman that furnished constant entertainment.

There were a couple of hundred passengers on that voyage. Everybody ate together, slept together and talked together in the one big room. Around the big open space in the center were the berths. They are not Pullman berths but merely spaces two feet wide and partitioned by an upright board. Chinese have the sensible habit of reclining while traveling. A boy brings a pot of tea and melon seeds for each passenger to munch. The passenger may recline and read or sit in his board bunk and watch what is going on in the center.

The jittery trip on the shallow waters of the Yellow River came to an end. At Ningsia I bade Father Depuyt farewell and crossed overland to see the flood devastation in Honan and talk to the people. In August, China's Sorrow—as the river is known because of its uncontrollable destructive floods—had risen almost without warning over its low banks in eastern Shensi. For fifteen hours it spilled forty thousand apprehensive and startled Chinese about in its turbulent waters.

From Ningsia north, then south around the great horseshoe bend through Shensi, the flood damage was comparatively light. Then, after the four-hundred-mile streamlined run south from the Great Wall, it hit a hairpin curve near the Honan border and spilled over the Honan plains.

The Franciscan missioner in charge of the Catholic mission at Ningsiang, two hundred miles above the bend, was an old man grown used to the erratic whims of China's Sorrow. He saw the flood waters surge past Ningsiang like a moving wall. Even here it was already loaded with a heavy silt, giving the rocks along the shore a coat of brown paint-like mud as it swept southward. The old Franciscan said he tried to get word down to his confreres at the hairpin bend and in Honan plain, so that they might spread the alarm. But the warnings didn't travel with the speed of the water—the Yellow River on rampage waits for no man. The wall of water struck the bend with the speed of a roaring express train. It hit the bank, rising six to one hundred feet high, then poured out over the plains, lashing and crumbling mud-brick homes, swamping fields, uprooting trees, destroying at least fifteen thousand men, women and children and unnumbered pigs and cattle, and ruining over fifty million dollars' worth of crops.

Everyone still alive had a hair-raising story to tell of his own individual experience with the waters. Clothes had been ripped off backs; women and youngsters caught unawares grabbed onto ridiculously small pieces of wood floating on the tide; pigs, people and chickens, all motivated by the same idea, climbed into well-rooted trees to escape the surging waters; one six-year-old youngster rode a bucking log and managed to keep it miraculously right side up in the crashing waters. A number of trees planted by soil conservationists saved many a life.

In the wake of the flood that wiped out crops and homes across the plain came the inevitable starvation and disease. In one city I passed through, the newspapers carried the account of a trial that was going on. A man accused of selling human flesh offered in his defense: "Dogs are feeding on the masses of corpses over the plains; should not people eat human flesh to keep alive?" The judge sorrowfully allowed the truth of this, but he sentenced the man for selling human flesh under the guise of horsemeat.

Three days after the wall of water had rolled across the countryside, Msgr. Thomas Megan of the Divine Word Fathers, who heads the Relief Committee in Loyang, started through the area of disaster and ruin. People huddled on high ground seemed dazed by the catastrophe. Children looked for their parents and parents for their children. Soup kitchens were organized for the penniless, and relief everywhere was struggling to meet the overwhelming need.

The flood was over, but the tears do not dry with the flood waters. Back the people must go, to where three feet of silt is added to their lands, and start over again in the bitterness of poverty. Relief organizations sent millions of dollars into the area to buy seed grain and give the victims a new start. They toiled and wept and shivered through the winter that followed, while the capricious Yellow River flowed calmly by once more. The church towers will go up again in another year and the bells will ring out the Angelus once more to halt the toil a moment for prayer.

We shall remember 1943 for the invasion of Italy, the Nazi retreat from Stalingrad, the first great bombings of German cities. But the people of Honan province will remember 1943 as the year of the locusts. Flood, famine, civil war and foreign invasion had already ravaged this unhappy province, but the scourge of grasshoppers was the most overwhelming calamity of all.

Msgr. Megan was riding his bicycle out toward the country one hot day in the early summer, when he saw villagers running madly from their homes toward the fields. He braked his wheel as he came abreast of a running farmer and asked what the excitement was all about. Hardly pausing, the farmer waved his arms and shouted, "The locusts are coming! The locusts are coming!" The missioner was to hear that cry repeated a thousand times that afternoon.

The locusts came like a cloud from the west, like a duststorm. They filled the air with a hum which the people dreaded more than that of Japanese bombers, for their devastation was universal and complete.

In the village, Msgr. Megan saw shopkeepers rush into the streets wiping their hands on their dirty aprons, and ricksha coolies stop dead and block the traffic, as all stared up at the invading aerial army that meant destruction for the autumn harvest. Old ladies that his bicycle barely missed as he wove through the crowd were lighting candles and joss sticks, jabbing them in clusters at each crossroad; devout Buddhists thumbed their beads in supplication; pious Catholic women begged him to pray, then fell to their knees and crossed themselves.

Cultivators of the fields ran to tie tassels of old rags to long poles. They went waving them over their crops to stop the enemy from landing, or to scare them away quickly. Pagan processions went through the fields, chanting prayers, waving banners, beating gongs and drums, striking cymbals and scattering mock money to placate the "devils." But it was all in vain, for the locusts kept landing by the millions.

Msgr. Megan rushed home through the storm of locusts that was darkening the sky. They struck against the façade of the cathedral like hailstones, as if through some peculiar instinct they must advance straight forward. On both sides the army rushed ahead, but those which dashed against the cathedral façade started slowly climbing to the top. This special detachment did not break ranks; they had to attain their objective in straight-line march. As they climbed the tower they looked like tremulous ivy in the wind. The air was filled with the hum of the diaphanous wings that sparkled in the sunlight.

After a few hours the futile resistance of the people was overcome. Some sat despondent by their fields and wept; others threw down their banners and joss sticks in disgust and started cursing the cruel fate that had given them flood and famine the year before and locusts this year. Helplessly they watched the wanton enemy ruin their crops, for locusts work fast. They land on a millet field in the evening, eat away every leaf, and by morning they have gone, leaving only skeleton stalks ready to die. The people saw them sweep down on their cornfields, eat away the tender leaves and the silks from the ears, and leave the naked worthless stalk swaying deserted in the next morning's breeze. The locusts raced through the beanfields eating the flowers, through the rows of cotton biting off the stem of the cotton bolls, through the fruit trees eating the stems while the fruit fell to the ground. What they actually eat is meager; what they destroy is measureless.

At the time, some of the newspaper correspondents went out from Chungking to report on the Honan disaster. On his return, Ted White of *Time* and *Life* told me, "That bishop is one of the greatest organizers and hardest workers I've ever seen." I wasn't surprised when the next issue of *Time* carried an account featuring the role played by Msgr. Megan.

The first foray moved swaths of destruction through the grain belt but left much. The females then stole off to the gullies and dry mountain streams and laid millions on millions of eggs in the sand. The arch villains passed—but the eggs throve. Within a few weeks a scavenging Youth Corps came hopping out of the mountains to destroy what the regulars had missed. As Msgr. Megan cycled about the countryside setting up relief kitchens, each turn of the wheel crushed dozens of the brittle insects flippantly parked in his path. And again the crows glutted themselves; blackbirds power-dived into the swarms, cramming their gullets full, and sparrows feasted on the crushed ones on the ground.

The people again fought with their poles and their prayers, and with fire and with water. But the locusts won. In some places, like the town of Hsuchang, which had been hard hit by the first invasion, the people tried to destroy the young locusts which could hop but not yet fly. Father Benoit, one of Msgr. Megan's assistants, reported how four thousand desperate peasants dug long, deep ditches and covered the bottoms with straw. Three thousand men, women and children chased the insects into the ditches. The other thousand people kept them in the corral, and when the ditch was nearly full the straw was fired. But even though millions of locusts were thus destroyed, it was as useless as fighting the tides. For one destroyed, a hundred lived. This second storm was so much greater than the first that ancient superstitious yarns gained credence. Old crones smoking long pipes went around telling the despairing people there was no good in killing locusts, for like the dragon's teeth, every one destroyed would bring millions more. Villagers, believing the locusts were some kind of spirits or gods to be propitiated, promised a great theatrical show in their honor if they would spare their fields and pass on to less devout parts of the country.

But the officials were more practical than the old ladies and offered a bounty of eight dollars a pound for locusts brought in. The people swatted, they burned, they smothered. They shot muzzle loaders into the swarms; they beat drums and gongs to scare them into nets. This helped morale, but that was about all.

After the second rampage the females again settled in the sand and dust of the roads, the dry river beds and loose soil of the fields, to deposit their eggs. In September a third army rallied.

The first two invasions had moved from east to west. This one went back from west to east, and what the two previous generations had missed was now attacked. But right in the midst of this last, most ravenous sortie, the pests for some unexplainable reason began to die off. They had defied all resistance and opposition that men could devise. It was perhaps the cold breath of September that blew on them, or some other stroke of nature that called a halt to the destroying hordes. On the corn tops, on the half-eaten leaves, in the trees and on the ground sprawled billions of dead locusts, strewn like the slain soldiers of a vanquished army—grotesque and gruesome, scattered over the battlefield.

But the people looked on apathetically: all during July, August and the first part of September they had seen their livelihood destroyed. Now the countryside lay as barren as a graveyard. The people knew that hunger and death would soon close in on them. The relief agencies and superhuman workers like Msgr. Megan did what they could, but it was little, in the face of total and general devastation. At least half the people of Honan—at least between seven and eight million—started a grim, pathetic hegira to the west. Their goal was fabulous Sinkiang, where the Chungking government offered them a new start. Only a few thousands reached their goal. How many dropped by the way, victims of hunger, disease and bandits, may never be known.

6 . . . Double Twins

DISASTER COMES AT THE END of so much Chinese history that it is pleasant now and then to reminisce over some case where a reasonable break in fortunes, plus human generosity and courage, produces a happy ending. One of the outstanding cases in my memory book is that of Chiu Shek-hoi, little mother of seven, four of whom arrived in the midst of bombardment.

The Japanese had landed at Bias Bay and were searing a path across country to Canton. Thousands of Chinese were trekking toward the great southern metropolis in the hope of finding means there to flee into the interior. Trotting along the road was a barefoot family. On a pole balanced from the father's shoulder were two baskets containing all he owned. In one of these baskets was cradled this man's youngest child. Following behind was his wife, with two more children hanging on to the blue pants the women wear in place of skirts. She waddled along slowly, heavy with pregnancy, and they stayed on the fringe of the milling crowd.

Soon they saw it would be useless to try to brave the pandemonium of the city, and they turned around. They bent their steps in the direction of Pokhoktung, where American doctors had a refugee camp and hospital.

It was a new experience for this mother of three to be going to a hospital. In China from time immemorial the midwife has taken the place of the doctor for childbirth. Childbirth is a natural function for the hard-working women, and they have their simple but efficient ways of dealing with it.

A few years ago on a mission visitation I arrived at a village with a Chinese who had worked with me for ten years as buyer, teacher, trouble-shooter and dabbler in prescribing native herbs and medicines. A young man whom I had married the year before met us with a worried look. He said his wife had been in labor all day without success and they were afraid she would die. My man Friday, who was the father of four children, started for the house with the young husband. Within half an hour he came back to say there was a new baby boy to baptize.

"Simple," he told me. "I gave that young fellow a few elementary instructions, and some directions to the midwife, and in a few minutes the baby was born."

But Chiu Shek-hoi, at the end of September, 1938, was up against something more complicated. One of the nurses present told us the blessed event caused more excitement than the Japanese bombs that shook the building from time to time. Not one but four new arrivals presented themselves. They came at half-hour intervals, a boy, a girl, another boy and another girl. The excited hospital staff improvised an incubator, and when they got time to give a little attention to the mother they found her weeping and asked her what was the matter.

"You told me the confinement cost for a baby was five dollars. Where am I going to get twenty dollars to pay for four of them?"

The doctor laughed and told her that there would be no charge, that the hospital should really pay *her* for such a performance.

Tension grew as the Japanese drew nearer. Babies and incubators were taken into air-raid shelters when the waves of bombers came over. They were carefully fed with medicine droppers, and they were held between life and death by a thread. But their squawking became lustier day by day, and during air raids frightened people said to the nurses that held the quads, "Stop noise, stop noise."

It came time for Mr. and Mrs. Chiu to give names to these babies born to the accompaniment of Japanese shells and bombs. They called them Kwok Keung, Kwok Ying, Kwok Kuen, Kwok Hing. The names mean Chiu of a Strong Country, Chiu of a Heroic Country, Chiu of a Powerful Country and Chiu of a Prosperous Country—otherwise, United States Chiu, Great Britain Chiu, Soviet Chiu and China Chiu.

After a time Mrs. Chiu went back to earning her living in the occupied city of Canton. Business was at a standstill and the going was hard. The Chius were people of the middle class who lived by buying and selling goods on a small scale. Old man Chiu was the type who liked to gather with cronies in the back of his shop, where he smoked a bamboo pipe so long he would have to put the taper between his toes to light it. He was a good-natured fellow who hadn't enough ambition to become a large merchant and hadn't enough industry to make money as a small one. Mrs. Chiu had the push of the family. With the help of some relief funds and her hard work they were able to struggle along and do quite well for the seven children. But she longed to get away from the Japanese. When the quads were past three, or about ready to be weaned, she thought the little rogues could stand travel. So Mr. Chiu packed two large round baskets half full with the family belongings. Then on top of the baggage he placed the quads, two in each basket. Mrs. Chiu took a basket with more baggage, and with the three other children walking, the family caravan started out.

They joined the periodic wave of refugees that left Canton for Free China. The Chinese language has no word for quadruplets, so they called them double twins. In each village where they passed the night, the double twins caused quite a commotion. People were good to them, and the missioners along the way gave them special attention.

After two weeks of weary journeying they came to the city of Kukong, where they met E. H. Lockwood of the Y. M. C. A., Chairman of the Relief Committee for that section and renowned for his work among refugees. Mr. Lockwood called up the governor's wife, Mrs. Lee, who was in charge of Kwangtung province's war orphanages, and she immediately came to see the quadruplets. She offered to take all the Chiu children into a "warphanage," but Shek-hoi flatly refused the offer. She said she wanted to find work, taking in washings or doing anything else to support her family and keep them together.

She found her way around in a few days and came to ask Mr. Lockwood to advance her a few hundred dollars to buy a mat shed. It was well located where she could start a little roadside stand and support the family, she thought. The money was advanced, and then Mr. Lockwood started to interest the government in the quads. He sent a wire to Mme. Chiang Kai-shek, whose secretary promptly wired back: "There is nothing in our budget for quadruplicates [*sic*]." Mr. Lockwood again approached the provincial government. Finally the Department of Civil Affairs provided the family with a house and an annual grant for the double twins.

After the family had moved and began to prosper, Shek-hoi went to thank Mr. Lockwood and repay the money advanced for the mat shed. He declined, saying the American people, through the United China Relief Fund, had adopted and helped the quads and would want to hold to their claim in bringing them up. She thanked him and soon brought around a snapshot of the double twins for the American people.

7 . . . The Jolly Roman

ONE DAY COLONEL DAVE BARRETT, U. S. Military Attaché, met me on the street in Chungking. He had just returned from Kweilin, where he had frequently visited Msgr. John Romaniello.

"Kweilin has taken him into the warmth of its civic heart, and any poll of the Kweilin citizenry would elect Monsignor Romaniello as Public Friend Number One," the colonel said. "The urchins playing in the street hop up to meet him; people riding past in rickshas hail him; merchants from their shop doors call out and get a familiar greeting in return."

There are few people there whom he does not know personally. His knowledge of them takes in the smallest incidentals —Ah-Shen's report card, Mei-Kwei's engagement, Ah Kung's (grandfather's) arthritis, or Ah Poh's (grandma's) dyspepsia. He drops into a store here, a dispensary there, the radio station or the hospital, and talks to every person about details of his home or family life.

Among the G.I.'s at airfields and camps around Kweilin, Msgr. Romaniello is known as the Jolly Roman.

The Jolly Roman's home takes on the aspect of an international club in the evening: a surprising variety of people are found there. Sometimes it's a coterie of fellow-missioners from farther afield who come in for a visit; sometimes G.I.'s in a truck or a jeep; sometimes General Chennault; sometimes a foreign or a Chinese businessman; sometimes one of the foreign correspondents. With the Monsignor as a kind of Master of Ceremonies in the house, everybody feels at ease.

Before the war Kweilin was a city of eighty thousand people. But as the Japanese invasion pushed into cities in North China, people found their way to Kweilin. It grew rapidly with the years, as the invaders took more and more territory. New factories, universities and schools, workshops and institutions sprang up. The railroad which was run to Kweilin, after the outbreak of the war in 1937, made it the jumping-off place for refugees. They came in freight-train loads from North China, and refugee camps clustered around the city. Kweilin had jumped to a population of half a million, and Msgr. Romaniello was on the jump with it.

The mission where he was became the focal point for the refugees. People instinctively flocked there from the trains, for they had always turned to the Catholic Mission in catastrophes of flood, famine and poverty in the past. Priests and lay people were assigned by the Monsignor to take care of these unfortunates driven from homes far away. Places were found for them in the refugee camps. Two priests were then sent to live in the camps with the refugees and take care of them. A general delivery post-office and clearing house was set up at the mission, and there the refugees received mail from friends on the road in other parts of China.

Monsignor visited the camps regularly to have a word with each family or each discouraged individual, to give them new hope. He found jobs for thousands of them, through his innumerable friends in the city; bought tools for the handicraft workers and started them back to making their own living; instituted new projects to employ them. He came to know everybody's qualifications so well that merchants sent word to him when they needed new hands to help them. The "Bishop's employment agency" became the talk of the town, and shopkeepers made and found new jobs for refugees, to co-operate with the Monsignor.

Monsignor's motto has always been, "Care for a man's hungry body and you'll win his soul."

In the spring of 1944 the refugee work in Kweilin had scaled down to a quiet routine. Father Robert Greene and Msgr. Romaniello were daily taking care of between three and four hundred needy refugees who came to the mission. Near the West Station at the outskirts of the city, one of the fathers was looking after the refugee camps. The American army boys, who came to Kweilin during 1943 and 1944 in considerable numbers, saw the American priests saying Mass for refugee crowds in theaters, sheds and any kind of makeshift shelter. Boys at the airfield dug deep into their pockets and collected enough to build a chapel. When the chapel was finished it was called Chapel of Our Lady of the Refugees. Later G.I. contributions built a large, bamboo-framed, thatched-roof chapel at the north gate, and this one was called St. Mary's of the Bamboo.

The missioners made their rounds through country villages in the spring of 1944. The farmers were plowing or pressing the rice plant seedlings into the soil. Perhaps the buzz of a few more planes did not alarm them, but whispers were reaching the farmers by "bamboo wireless" that the Japanese were concentrating troops to drive on Changsha. The papers began to carry toned-down reports of Japanese plans. Refugees came to ask Msgr. Romaniello what he thought of the danger, since Changsha was only a few hundred miles from Kweilin.

Then one morning the Japanese advanced, and evacuation of Changsha was ordered. This meant that thousands of refugees would soon come pouring in, and work at high pressure would be needed again. Monsignor organized his staff of priests and workers and plowed into the job. Father McCabe in Chuanchow, a hundred miles nearer Changsha, got the first wave of refugees and was overwhelmed with the task. The Jolly Roman thrives on maddening activity, and he went up to share the work with him. But within the month the Japanese had taken Changsha and were pressing on toward Hengyang.

Monsignor knew that Kweilin would be the next big city on the list, so he left Father McCabe to work until the last minute there and went home to help with the Kweilin evacuation.

Japanese bombers were already slipping in to bomb Kweilin, and between raids Msgr. Romaniello gathered up his belongings and moved to a boat on the Foo River. He wanted to have a place ready to carry on, if his mission were destroyed again. The Chinese saw him moving and were afaid he was going home when they needed him so much.

"This is my home," he told them from the houseboat, and started operating his dispensaries and rice lines from the water front, farther away from the danger zone of bombing.

The order for evacuation of Kweilin came in July, 1944, but Monsignor stayed on until Kweilin became a dead, empty city. For weeks porters were seen carrying boxes, suitcases, duffle bags, trying to find a place on a freight train, truck or boat.

The Jolly Roman got a "carryall" and two men to help him from the American army. He went to the refugee camps and through the streets to pick up deserted, penniless people, too weak or too poor to get to the overcrowded freight trains. The trains would be packed and no more people permitted through the gates, but the Jolly Roman would tell the railroad officials, "These are friends of mine," and each load found its way to the train. He would go to the freight cars, where every conceivable spot was crowded with people, and ask them to take the baggage and help up the people he had brought. Then he'd hand them enough money to buy food on their way to the safer interior.

The dreary life of the refugees, waiting hours for the freight trains to start, was brightened by the repeated appear-

ance of the Monsignor and his friends. They'd see him get
past the smiling guards again and again with his dozen or so
"friends," and somehow found place to squeeze his friends
on the train. Each time they saw the army "carryall" coming
toward the station, the word went up and down the crowded
train, "It's the Monsignor and another load of friends."

Until one has seen refugees, forced to leave by evacuation
orders, swarming over a train, one does not understand the
word crowded. Living humans clung to the engine like barna-
cles; they formed an umbrella over the coal car; they piled on
top of the cars in clusters of human flesh; they threw boards
across the rods to ride between the wheels; they clung to the
steel ladder rungs on the side. A mass of human heads and
hands made the train invisible as it started to creep away.
Twenty thousand people were being moved out daily from
Kweilin.

The Jolly Roman and Father Greene were watching a train
ready to pull out one day when a child voice called them. At
their feet was a little tot that they knew, sobbing because she
had lost her mother on the train. Monsignor took the child in
his arms and hoisted her up to one of his parishioners on the
train, with instructions to find the child's parents at one of the
stops. He slipped something into the child's hand for sweets
as he walked beside the moving train.

"*Hsieh, hsieh, Tsu-Chiao!* Thank you, thank you, Monsignor," the child called, smiling before the tears were dry. His
own eyes filled as he waved good-by to the child and his
parishioners and friends leaving Kweilin.

The Jolly Roman ignored evacuation orders and stayed
until the civilian population was out. Then he took his bicycle
and rode through the ghost town, as silent and deserted as it
had been during the air-raid alarms. The army was burning
the installations at the airfield and planting demolition bombs.
Msgr. Romaniello sent his priests on trucks with the American

army boys toward Kweiyang, four hundred miles in the interior. He himself went out with the officers to a plane just before the field was blown up. His plan was to fly to Chungking and arrange with the Relief Committee for large grants of funds, then go down and assist the refugees at the end of the railroad.

In Chungking the American Advisory Committee and Anglican Bishop Hall with the British Committee on Relief made generous grants, and the Monsignor was ready to start back.

Walking down the streets of Chungking with Kweilin's beloved Monsignor, I felt as if I were accompanying a movie star. Some of the thousands he had helped through Kweilin had arrived there, and people were waving, bowing or running across the street to greet him at every few steps. When he stopped to talk to a group of Chinese, crowds flocked around. They stood gaping at the strange scene of a jolly foreigner carrying on a conversation in fluent Chinese; finally the cops chased them away to let traffic pass.

We met an American aviator on the street, and Monsignor told him he was about ready to start back to the refugee work in Kwangsi.

"I'm flying to Kunming with a transport in the morning, and I'll take you; from there you can get one of the many planes flying back to Liuchow, Kwangsi," the captain said.

After the plane landed at Kunming, the Jolly Roman was talking to another officer when General Chennault saw him. The general took him by the arm and led him into his office for a chat. When he learned that the Monsignor wanted to go back to Kwangsi he pressed a button. The aide appeared, and General Chennault said, "Fix up a ticket for Monsignor Romaniello to go to Liuchow on the first plane out."

Msgr. Romaniello spent several days in Liuchow placing his priests strategically at different points through which the

refugees must pass. The center which eventually caught them
all was Chin Ts'eng Chiang on the Kwangsi-Kweichow border,
and to this hot spot went Msgr. Romaniello himself. He found
the problems many and complex. The work would have been
a challenge to giants. After ten days of putting up sheds, medical dispensaries and rice kitchens, he was once again low on
funds. Getting into an army truck he bumped over the mountain roads for three days on his way back to Chungking.

Between spells of arranging for relief funds he managed
to tell us something about this last and most harrowing of all
refugee migrations. Chin Ts'eng Chiang means Gold River
City. It is a town on the Kwangsi border where a clear blue
river comes tumbling out of the mountain province of Kweichow. At some time in the dim past, people gathered here to
pan gold, and when the town grew they called it Gold River
City. As they retreated from the Japanese in North China, the
Chinese took up hundreds of miles of railroad, with which they
laid new stretches in the south. When the line reached Gold
River City in 1941, bringing the first of many waves of refugees, the place quickly took on the appearance of an actual
frontier gold-rush town. Save for the railroad hotels and one
or two other buildings, it was a community of hastily thrown
up bamboo mat sheds with thatched roofs—a city of transients
waiting for the railroad to be built another hundred miles
farther.

The Japanese push into Changsha and Hengyang during
the summer of 1944 drove refugees before it like locusts, and
twenty to thirty thousand arrived daily in Gold River City.
There were no accommodations for them; most of them
dumped their few poor belongings in the fields and slept under
the stars. Those who had some funds started buying bamboo
poles, mats, grasses and leaves from the country farmers near
by, and the city of mat sheds resumed its magic growth. These
sheds were three-walled, open-front, grass-roof constructions.

They kept out most of the rain, some of the wind and all the sun. The passageways between the rows of sheds were clay mud, dusty when the season was dry, oozy when the rains came.

Business and industry increased. The barber, the baker and the tailor set up shop. The storekeepers bought merchandise from the country folk and sold it from their mat sheds. Those who could afford it put peanut oil in a saucer, with a wick hanging lighted over the edge, for illumination. The mat shed town was an eerie sight in the evening. In the flickering glow of the saucer lights, people could be seen sleeping in their open-front sheds. A few were on boards, most of them on the ground. In the fields beyond, where thousands dwelt without roof or light, the people lay huddled in fitful rest on the rough earth. Dogs barked; babies cried, and now and then there was the sound of funeral wailing.

Msgr. Romaniello found Gold River City a madhouse of confusion, a place of filth and squalor, suffering and death. People were dying everywhere from hunger, exposure and exhaustion. There was no provision for coffins—the dead were dropped into the Gold River at night. As new waves of refugees poured in, the crowds milled around, talked until they were exhausted, then fell down to sleep wherever they happened to be, their heads on their baggage. Even the frequent rain failed to make them stir.

Msgr. Romaniello and the two padres assisting him used a big one-room shed as a chapel for Mass in the morning; as a dining room at meal times; as a dispensary in caring for the sick who formed queues daily, seeking medicine or treatment; as an office for giving help or advice, and as a bedroom when the long day was done. Over half the people were sick with dysentery, fevers and coughs. A few Chinese doctors and nurses had come as refugees, and Monsignor hired them. They worked with the fathers all day, eating only two meals, which they prepared themselves, one before they started work at eight-thirty, the other after they quit at five. A few cases of typhoid and cholera broke out, and Msgr. Romaniello had to leave his post to fetch more medicines and vaccines from Kweiyang in an army truck. After that, he established a "Death House." When there was little hope of recovery, the patients were carried to the shed near the dispensary.

The fathers carried a medical kit, one part filled with medicines, one part with money wrapped in paper. After breakfast they would make the rounds of the city, caring for the sick and the hungry. The sick were given medicine. Destitute, hungry families were handed some of the wrapped-up money, which they could take without embarrassment.

A refugee baker threw up a stall beside the lines of waiting patients near the priests' mat shed, but found they were too poor to buy his bread or cakes. Msgr. Romaniello asked him, "How many cakes and loaves of bread have you?"

"About two hundred," the baker answered.

The Jolly Roman gave him a big encouraging wink and said, "Why not give them away, if you can't sell them?"

The baker caught on and passed along the line of hungry refugees, giving a loaf to each. Dollars sent from bakers and candlestick makers in America were used to reimburse this poor but generous dough-mixer in China.

The Chinese have perhaps the finest sense of humor in the world, and flickers of light and laughter break through the darkest grief. American soldiers, trudging along the road past the weary, hungry masses, would remark on this as people shouted, *"Teng Hao!* You're tops!"—or the only English word they knew, "Okay"—with light-hearted smiles.

And with this humor went great generosity. At mealtime, bowl and chopsticks were lent to those who had none. Mothers poked rice from their bowl into the mouths of children they had never seen before.

For a few weeks the work in Gold River City went along well enough under the circumstances. Relief agencies put up rows of mat sheds to shelter the homeless, organized new medical units and brought in supplies of food and medicine.

Then one morning a train-whistle screamed warning up the valley: it was an extra train, bringing refugees and word that the Japanese were on the move again. As word spread that the enemy had started rolling north from Liuchow and was heading for Gold River City, panic spread through the multitudes. The people milled around in the mud, forming worried, excited groups or packing up their belongings. And on every lip was the question, "What next? Where to, now?"

For although the railroad had been laid a few score miles farther into Kweichow province, trains rarely made the trip. The few available trains brought the refugees as far as Gold River, dumped them and went back for more. Just the same, the scared migrants now filled the station, lined the sidings and slept by the tracks, waiting and hoping as only the Chinese know how to wait and hope. On the sidings were hundreds of freight cars which the refugees used as homes: clothes and firewood, pots and pans, lay scattered over the roofs of these cars and hung down their sides.

In the midst of this new chaos, disease became rampant. The town's environs had long since taken on the aspect of a litter-covered meadow. With no provision for sanitation, the ground was drenched in filth like a gigantic barnyard, and the stench was almost unbearable.

In this crisis the American army came to the assistance of Msgr. Romaniello. After the Jolly Roman had made a plea at a near-by camp, G. I.'s came out with jeeps and trucks and picked up the children, the aged and the sick that the missioner pointed out. The army lads lifted those who needed lifting and went out of their way to carry luggage.

"The men with the trucks always seemed to find room for

one more when they came across someone who had fainted or
fallen by the roadside," said Msgr. Romaniello. "I saw an army
doctor stop his ambulance and get out and treat a refugee who
had fallen off a truck and cut his scalp; then he took him along
in the ambulance." Many a weary mother, plodding through
the mud with a baby strapped to her back, was picked up by
the Yanks.

Monsignor described a typical family in the parade of fleeing people. Balanced on one end of a bamboo pole slung
across his shoulder the father had the family's quilt and bedding; on the other, the rest of their possessions—rice, pots,
shoes. Behind him walked his wife with a baby in her arms.
Holding on to her clothes was a child of seven.

Some families pooled their strength and put their belongings on a cart. Two men were pulling and two pushing one
cart which was piled high with baggage. On top of the baggage were three little laughing babies, blissfully ignorant of
the tragedy in which they were taking part. The Monsignor,
riding in a jeep, asked the driver to stop and pressed a paper
packet of money in each of the babies' hands.

Next in the parade was a youngster leading a horse with
three small children perched on its back. The father and
mother walked alongside carrying the baggage. Monsignor ran
out by jeep to the first railroad stop beyond Gold River City.
In this place, too, refugees were living in freight cars shunted
off on sidings, and in one car a crowd was packed on top of a
load of bombs. He recognized two girls from his parish in
Kweilin. They told him they had been there ten days, waiting
for the train to move on. One had been seriously ill with
dysentery. He loaded them into the jeep, took them back to
Gold River, and there found an army truck to take them to the
interior. A few days later the trainload of bombs was blown up
by Japanese planes.

The hundred thousand refugees were nearly cleared out of

Gold River as the Japanese approached, and Msgr. Romaniello and his priests moved back fifty miles to Tushan. Within two weeks they were forced to move again. The Japanese columns were coming once more.

8 . . . Enemies Without and Within

IN THE EARLY WINTER OF 1944, Chungking was stirring with activity. The crisis was approaching and the outcome was uncertain. Kweiyang, two days away by car, had been evacuated as the Japanese neared its outskirts. Chungking residents packed their bags and baskets and left the city by boat, by truck and afoot, realizing that another Nanking might be their fate if the capital were taken by the messengers of the New Order.

Just at this time, when Chungking was facing its greatest threat from the invading foreign army, Chinese Communist headquarters at Yenan began stabbing at Chungking in a violent radio and press campaign.

The Communist dissenters, after years of fighting against the Central Government, had finally established themselves at Yenan. Since 1928, when Chiang Kai-shek broke with them, they had held out against Chiang's army. General Chu Teh at that time gathered his mobs of soldiers and Red sympathizers and retired into Kiangsi Province, where they proclaimed a state of armed insurrection and set up soviets. Busy wiping out local and provincial generals in his continuing struggle to unite China, Chiang was not able to defeat the Kiangsi Communists until 1935, when the Red Army's remnants made their famous ten-thousand-mile trek to the northwest. Some twenty priests were caught in the Communist backsweep: some escaped, some were ransomed and two were killed.

The march of destruction and pillage ended in 1936, when

Mao Tse-tung, the Communist party leader, and Red General Chu Teh set up a "Chinese Soviet Republic" in the northern part of Shensi province, with Yenan as the capital. Chiang Kai-shek now offered to stop attacking the Communists, provided they agreed to place their armed forces under his command; abolish the "Soviet Republic"; give allegiance to the Nanking government, and cease anti-Nanking propaganda, confiscation of lands and all other manifestations of the class struggle.

The Communists accepted the terms, but after Japan hurled her armies into the north of China in July, 1937, the Reds' pledges didn't mean much. In September, 1944, I spent three-quarters of an hour with War Minister Ho in Chungking, and he showed me documented proof of how every promise made in 1937 had been broken: how General Chu Teh and Mao Tse-tung had persisted in their independent policy—seizing more and more territory, collecting their own taxes, printing their own money, making their own laws and, in short, continuing non-co-operation with Chiang Kai-shek.

But the Communists, though well entrenched in Shensi, had not previously been considered a serious threat to Chiang's National Government. It was argued that the Chinese communists represented only one-fifth of one per cent of the nation's inhabitants: according to the party's own figures, membership is only nine hundred thousand. The area under Communist control was one-fiftieth of the area of all China and was confined to a border region in the northwest. The Yenan regime controlled thirty-two counties, of which twenty-one had been taken over since 1939, or long after the 1937 agreement and during the struggle against Japan.

There were those who called Chiang's government dictatorial and reactionary, but observers of long residence, familiar with the intricacies of Chinese resurgence, could see no substitute for the authoritarian Chungking regime; at least not while the country had a powerful enemy at its throat. Chiang's authority was far less complete in effect than that of President Roosevelt or Prime Minister Winston Churchill under the wartime powers granted them by their democratic electors.

In any case, our relations with China became so bad in 1944 that the war effort was being hindered. The climax came when the news reports said that General Stilwell under orders from Washington urged that Chungking make peace with the Communists and that both the Red and National forces be placed under his command. Chiang resented this, considering it an infringement of China's sovereignty and a reflection on his statesmanship. The general left in September. Ambassador Gauss told me soon after that he would like to resign. Resign he did, and the new ambassador, Patrick Hurley, came to Chungking. It was not long before he sent home all officials who were not supporters of the Chiang Kai-shek regime.

The vigorous, optimistic Hurley decided late in October to fly to Yenan, where he pleaded with the Communists to come to an agreement with the Central Government in the hour of danger. He succeeded in bringing Chou En-lai back to Chungking for talks with Chiang. Chou said he came with plenipotentiary powers, and the conversations were begun. They were still continuing a month later, when it became clear the Japanese were in a fair way to advance as far as Chungking itself. The closer the enemy came, the slower the negotiations grew.

The crisis came to the capital in the first week of December. The Japanese had surrounded the outskirts of Kweiyang, and its fall was expected momentarily. Residents of Chungking continued their flight from the capital—for it seemed certain the enemy would be at the gates by Christmas. Even the government was preparing to move. Foreign Office workers told us that clerks had gone to Lanchow and Western Szechuan to arrange for government office space.

Trucks loaded with troops and supplies rumbled through

the city day and night. The rumor was current that an agreement had been reached at last between the Central Government and the Communists and that the one hundred thousand men who had been immobilized in the north would be thrown into the defense of Kweiyang. For, as the Generalissimo told his war minister, Ho Yin Ching—who was ordered to hold the city under pain of death—"Chungking stands or falls by Kweiyang." But it was precisely in this hour of acute danger and near panic that Chou En-lai, the Yenan delegate, announced he did not have plenipotentiary powers after all and flew back to Yenan, the Little Moscow. That was the end of the Chungking-Yenan negotiations, and it marked the beginning of an intensive radio propaganda campaign in which the Reds, apparently sure the Central Government would flee, tried to rally the people of China against Chiang Kai-shek.

In the midst of this gloom, Msgr. Romaniello came up from Kweiyang one night with a truckload of American soldiers, a demolition squad that had been planting dynamite on airfields and ammunition dumps as the Allies retreated from the Japanese. We gave the tired men a hot meal and they spread their bedding on the dining-room floor. When we asked them how close the enemy was, they said advance patrols had taken the railhead at Tuyun, a town a few miles east of Kweiyang which sat astride the supply route from Kunming and the Burma and Stilwell roads.

"Well, we hope you are not here to blow up Chungking," we said, and the men didn't laugh. They shook their heads doubtfully and one of them muttered, "We don't know."

The following morning, in conversation at the little hospital attached to United States Army headquarters, General Albert C. Wedemeyer, the new commander-in-chief, expressed concern over the fate of missioners in the path of the advancing Japanese. Then he invited me into his office and traced a long forefinger over a war map. "The situation is serious," he said. "In fact, we must be prepared to evacuate Chungking. Tomorrow we are starting to move part of our headquarters to Kunming. We'll make a last ditch stand there, if we have to."

But the Japanese did not approach Chungking. They did not even attack Kweiyang. For at this moment, to the amazement of us all, they suddenly started pulling back their over-extended armies. American forces had taken Saipan and were fast building airfields from which the B-29's would strike at the Japanese homeland. It would do the Japanese no particular good, now, to knock out American bases in the interior of China or to force the Chinese Government out of Chungking, the last citadel of Chiang's prestige (this would merely throw support to the Communists, and the Japanese aim naturally was to keep China divided).

As the Japanese were nearing Chungking, the Yenan radio blared in a campaign against the "capitalistic, reactionary, landlord, dictatorial" government in Chungking; it announced the Shensi Soviets had formed a committee of liberation for China—thinking the Chungking government was finished. It was then that the Japanese suddenly halted their advance. The Communist stand during the crisis made the resumption of negotiations seemingly impossible.

Ambassador Hurley did not give up hope for an eventual reconciliation between the Reds and the recognized government of China. I visited him just before I left Chungking in January and asked him if he wasn't discouraged.

"No," he said. "There is still hope."

In February, Chou En-lai did come back for conversations, and he came with new demands. This did not astonish Chiang Kai-shek but it did somewhat surprise and irk General Hurley, who was responsible for the attempted rapprochement. A government official told me what everyone knew, that the Communists do not want a settlement with the National Government.

"Such a settlement would take away their greatest weapon," he said. "Their hope for power is turmoil, trouble and division."

In 1944, Father Cormack Shannahan of the Passionists, representing *The Sign* magazine, joined a group of newsmen who had been invited to visit Yenan. All missioners had been driven out in 1936 and the Cathedral had been taken over by the Communists. Father Shannahan asked if he could hold services for the people who had been deprived of priests for eight years. Making a gesture for the benefit of the foreign press, the Communists agreed.

But later, when communicants came toward the priest to go to confession, Red soldiers barred their way with rifles. "No private conversations allowed," they said.

"But this is part of their religious practice—a practice that is world-wide," said Father Shannahan.

"Not here," snapped the Communist officer. "The people can tell us and we can relate to you whatever they have to say."

6 . . . "In Life, All of Us—"

It was ten years in January since I left America to come to China the last time, and my decennial furlough was due. I called on General Wedemeyer to inquire about priority for passage to America.

"Since you are working with the Army I think it can be arranged," he told me.

He radioed Washington and the answer came back next day: "Approved."

General Wedemeyer talked with me a long time that day. He has the look of a soldier—sparkling eyes, gray hair, soldierly straight but not militarily severe. After a short time in China, he seemed to have an excellent grasp of the situation and the war needs there. He had the unenviable task of succeeding a very popular soldier, General Joseph W. Stilwell. Vinegar Joe, as he is called, knew China as he knew his military manual. He loved the din of battle and wanted to be tramping and fighting with his beloved infantry at the front.

I prepared for the plane flight to America by saying au revoir to friends in Chungking. Among the round of farewell parties, the most appreciated was a tea party given by the distinguished Chinese Bishop Paul Yupin, who had recently returned from America. The Christian General Feng Yu-hsiang gave a speech, then autographed a little verse he wrote out in Chinese. It translates:

"Above and below the heavens all are one family,
In life, all of us are brothers."

The plane route was across India and Africa, but I made arrangements to stop in Rome.

Colonel Lacy made a special landing on the field at Rome to let me out. Because I was the first clergyman to come to the Eternal City from China in many years, I was granted a private audience with Pope Pius XII.

What impressed me most about the Holy Father was the great serenity of his face. I had half-expected he would wish to converse in French, but he addressed me instead in faultless English. He spoke in a soft voice ringing with sincerity, and every now and then his face would light up with a smile that was calm and radiant. After discussing war conditions and their effect on the missions in China, he spoke at some length of the problems and misfortunes of the church throughout the wartorn world. But his voice remained calm and his countenance unruffled throughout the interview, which he closed with his benediction.

I spent two weeks in sad, hungry Rome, visiting with various churchmen and renewing my acquaintance with the historic wonders of the city. One day when I was being shown through the museum of St. John Lateran by Father Schulien of the Divine Word Fathers, an anthropologist of international repute, we came to a priceless model of a Chinese temple, about six feet high. "Only a little while ago this temple was the hiding-place of a Chinese priest," Father Schulien said with an enigmatic smile. And so I learned one more story of Chinese courage and resourcefulness in this age of war.

His name is Father Li—pronounced "Lee." He was a member of the Capuchin order, and he was helping out in a church at Naples during the German occupation. He was allowed to visit a prisoner-of-war camp near by, and one day the Germans arrested him—accused him of having helped some British and Americans to escape.

Father Li was tried, convicted and put in prison: he was to

be shot the following day. But that night American bombers came over and a direct hit blasted open the prison where he was held. He recovered consciousness to find he was lying in a heap of rubble with clouds of smoke and dust floating between him and the bright Mediterranean stars. Surprisingly, he was not hurt, and he escaped to a village in the hills.

Here, protected by friendly peasants, he evolved a plan for getting back to Rome. He got his friends to dress him in a garb which the average Nazi would take for a Japanese ki-mono. Posing as the wife of a member of the Japanese Embassy staff in Rome, he went back into Naples and asked a German convoy officer for transportation to Rome. It was a harrowing ride for Father Li. One of the soldiers took an interest in the supposed Madame Butterfly and tried to make love. The priest, scared to death lest he be discovered and shot by the side of the road, stalled the Nazi off by agreeing to meet him at a certain street corner in Rome that night. Father Li was dropped off a little distance from the Japanese Embassy, and as soon as the truck was out of sight he made for the Capuchin Fathers' house.

The Capuchins dared not shelter their condemned con-frere for fear of German searching parties. But Father Schulien, who had been courted by the Nazis because of his reputation as a scientist, and who had repeatedly rebuffed their offers, took on Father Li as a helper in the Lateran Museum. And when-ever German visitors or possible searching parties entered the vast halls, Father Li lifted up the slide of his hiding place in the little temple and was out of sight.

In May, 1944, peeping from the Lateran Museum windows, Father Li saw the German trucks and tanks leave Rome. Then he was able to take up residence in the Capuchin house. When I talked to him and a group of Chinese student priests, they were trying to find transportation to their native land.

Thus, whether it is a Mongolian boy leading a camel

around the earth, or a Chinese friar posing as a Japanese woman to outwit the Wehrmacht, or a half-armed rabble defending its last mountain passes against the enemy invaders of her country, old China goes on.